Fly Fishing:
Simple to Sophisticated

A New, Systematic Approach for
Catching More Trout on a Fly

Al Kyte

Illustrations by Linnea Wigren
Photographs by Van Rackages
Cover Photographs by Sashi Nakamoto
Cover Design by Diana J. Goodin

Leisure Press
P.O. Box 3
West Point, N.Y. 10996

To George P. Dozier
Who took the time to pass his love
of fly fishing on to me

To Barbara, Bertha and Al Kyte, Sr.
Who cared enough to encourage its
further development

To John and Tamara
With whom I can share this love

A publication of Leisure Press.
P.O. Box 3, West Point, N.Y. 10996
Copyright © 1982 Leisure Press
All rights reserved. Printed in the U.S.A.

Library of Congress Number: 81-86515
ISBN 0-88011-027-9

CONTENTS

ABOUT THE AUTHOR

FLY FISHING: Simple to Sophisticated

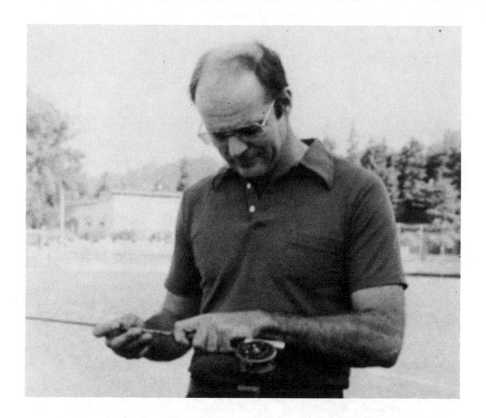

Al Kyte holds a Doctorate degree from the Berkeley Campus of the University of California where he is highly regarded as a faculty member in the department of physical education. In addition to teaching physical activity and theory classes, he has coached two sports and has been elected to statewide office in his professional organization. As an undergraduate at Cal he played a year of basketball under the legendary Pete Newell and was an All-Conference first baseman in baseball. By that time he had already been fly fishing for ten years.

Almost thirty years later he has combined his love of fly fishing with his love for teaching. His recreational fly casting class fills to capacity each term with university students and his fly fishing classes offered through University Extension fill with adults from all walks of life. He also teaches in the prestigeous Fenwick Fly Fishing Schools, is a licensed fishing guide in California and contributes instructional articles to fly fishing magazines. A popular speaker, he is frequently invited to present programs to fly fishing clubs on topics such as nymph fishing, aquatic entomology and reading the water.

Preface

This is a book about fly fishing — for trout. I have written it for readers much like myself, who stalk the pages of such books for practical fishing ideas, and don't appreciate having to wade through volumes of prose for each tidbit. I enjoy well-rendered prose, but not when mixed with my fly fishing. What this book lacks in personal accounts of battles with huge trout, it should make up for in a logical and concise presentation of fly fishing concepts.

I have organized this book quite differently from most instructional books of fly fishing. Almost universally, such books contain chapters on the obvious dimensions of the sport—the trout, equipment, casting, reading the water, entomology, dry fly fishing, wet fly and nymph fishing, streamer fishing, lake fishing, and playing and landing trout.

This typical organization of other books makes sense but it's hard to apply in real fishing situations that you and I actually encounter on lakes or streams. Although such handbooks supply information on how to fish, they leave the learner dangling as to *when* to apply *which* techniques or concepts. For example, when you first find yourself fishing in cascading water, which specific comments from the chapter on tackle and rigging apply, which casting variations are useful, which of the comments about dry fly or nymph fishing are appropriate, and which of the many problems in playing big fish are most likely to be experienced? The content simply has not been organized to put these elements together for you.

The absence of such an integrated approach is what my fly fishing students say they have been missing in the instructional books in our sport. It is what I have aimed to provide in writing this book.

I start my "integrated approach" in Chapter 2 after providing some basic information on equipment, rigging up, fly casting, and trout and its environment. Chapters 2 through 11 each cover one fairly distinctive fly fishing method or practical fishing "program" in sequence from simple to sophisticated, though any such ordering is arbitrary to a degree. At least the beginning chapters, especially Chapters 2 and 3 are quite basic, but the last four or five assume the reader already has some fly fishing experience.

The integration of content should be even more apparent within a chapter, because each chapter is presented in the same way, by means of identical sub-headings. Whether each fly fishing method is unique or is similar to other methods becomes apparent through this ordering. Thus each method is described in terms of the following sub-headings:

- **The fishing situation:** water type, problems for the angler, distinctive characteristics of the trout or its food;

- **Rigging adaptations:** modifications or departures from the basic general-purpose rigging described in Chapter 1;

- **The approach:** the role of observation, concealment and angle of approach;

- **Casting techniques:** variations or specialty casts appropriate to the fishing method;

- **Line-handling and fishing techniques:** specific things you do when the fly is in the water;

- **Hooking and landing the fish:** tips on detecting strikes, setting the hook, and playing the trout that may be distinctive to the fishing method;

- **Wading and safety:** wading equipment, wading techniques, and safety concerns pertinent to this method or habitat;

- **Selected references:** most helpful sources pertaining to the content presented in the chapter.

So the whole idea is to insert a particular piece of content in that part of the book that describes conditions where it is most useful. The tuck cast, for example, is not introduced until I describe a short-line, wet-fly method that is appropriate to its use. If you are beginning fly fisher, you probably benefit most from this presentation of content *as you need it.* However, if you feel the need to know more about some of the basic concepts, I suggest you use this book as a cross-reference with one or more of the traditional handbooks for beginners. Such books do not include information for experienced fly fishers (as this one does), so they have room for expanded discussions of equipment selection, knot-tying, trout foods, and other basic concepts. For such cross-referencing I recommend *Scientific Anglers Fly Fishing Handbooks* and Anderson's *The Curtis Creek Manifesto* because they are usually available, inexpensive, and comprehensive in scope. Other larger books, such as Joe Brooks' *Trout Fishing,* provide even more thorough coverage of basic material.

If you are already experienced at fly fishing, you should find the last half of this book more appealing. You have already read chapters on casting, equipment, reading the water, and fishing techniques, and have fished several of the methods described. The material with which to cross-reference this book is already in your head. So the first part of the book will give order to many of the things you already do, and perhaps enable you to apply them in different situations. The last four or five chapters should give you more advanced concepts to experiment with in your fishing. If you are quite advanced, this book will provide a logical and practical way to convey your skill and knowledge to others.

To the extent that I am successful in what I have set out to do, I give much of the credit to the combined artistry of Linnea Wigren, Van Rackages, and Sashi Nakamoto. I think you will agree that the essential beauty of Linnea's drawings and the clarity of Van's photographs make it possible for you to visualize some of the more abstract concepts I have tried to communicate. And Sashi Nakamoto, my "guide" on Lake

Pyramid, reveals his artistic ability in the cover photographs. If you are fortunate enough to catch trophy trout, it is nice indeed when the skilled angler next to you happens to be an art director with his camera in tow.

I am also indebted to a willing and capable group of angler-editors including Bob Dering, Scott Henderson, Frank Collin and Chet Murphy. The streams they fish are a good deal clearer than the manuscript they waded through.

Over the last 35 years, I have been quite fortunate in the fly fishermen I have known. Their willingness to share their knowledge and skill has undoubtedly contributed to the content of this book. First and foremost was George P. Dozier, a skilled dry fly angler of freestone streams, who I was fortunate enough to have for my uncle. A great man and an ideal fishing companion, he made the sport a fantastic adventure for a young boy—an adventure that becomes an obligation to transmit to others. In effect, he gave me years of free lessons on reading water and fishing with dry flies.

Others who have personally shared their expertise, in order of their appearance, were Paul Needham (the trout and its environment), Cal Bird (fly fishing, fishing spots), E.H. "Polly" Rosborough (fly tying, nymphing, fishing spots), Dick Holland (nymphing, streamer fishing, big fish habits), Ted Fay (wet fly fishing, fishing spots), Andre Puyans (fly tying, meadow stream dry fly fishing), Howell Daly and Vince Resh (aquatic entomology) Frank Collin (fly tying, dry fly fishing), Charles Brooks (nymphing, fishing spots), Bob Howe (fly tying, nymphing), Mel Krieger (fly casting, equipment), and Hal Janssen (still water fly fishing, equipment modifications). The personal interaction with these experts has been at least as rewarding as the concepts they have shared.

Other men have contributed important ideas to my fly fishing perspective without making personal appearances. These include Al McClane (perspective on the sport), Jim Leisenring (wet fly fishing), Chuck Fothergill (nymphing), G.E.M. Skues and Frank Sawyer (nymphing), Hartt Wixom (big fish habits), Vince Marinaro (meadow-stream dry fly fishing, fly tying), Al Troth (fly tying), George Harvey (equipment modifications), Lefty Kreh (fly casting and equipment modifications), Brian Clarke (still water fly fishing), and most recently, Joe Humphreys (nymphing).

In a very real sense, you will be learning from these teachers as you read this book and apply its concepts.

1
GETTING READY TO GO FLY FISHING
Some Basic Essentials

If you are new to the sport of fly fishing, there are things you will need to know before your first day on the water. You will have to know how to select equipment, assemble it, and use it—how to cast. Also, you will profit by knowing something about your quarry, the trout, and its environment. Such basics, which are covered briefly in this chapter, transcend the various styles or methods of fly fishing described throughout the remainder of the book.

If you have not done so already, take a few moments to read the preface. There I've laid out this book's unusual organization and explained how it is intended to assist you—whether you have fly fished before or not.

Selection of Equipment

In this book, I have described a variety of fly fishing methods—some that work best in rather small streams, and others that are definitely big river techniques. Still others pertain to catching trout in lakes. All are methods for catching trout on an artificial fly. No one fly rod will be perfectly suited to all of these methods. However, if you are a beginner with limited funds for purchasing equipment, you may want to select one general-purpose fly rod that will adequately cover this range of habitat.

The fly rod I recommend for general trout use is 8½ feet long and is designed to cast a number 6 fly line. If expense is a limiting consideration, I would further suggest that the fly rod be made of fiberglass, though an increasing number of people are discovering that it is fun to fish with graphite because of its light feel. The expense of obtaining a graphite rod (or a fiberglass one for that matter) can be cut considerably by building (finishing) your own rod; your local tackle-shop dealer should be able to get you started.

Many of the better-selling fly rods are built for such general trout use and feature what is termed a "progressive" action. Though stiff in the butt, these rods are progressively more flexible (less stiff) toward the tip. This smooth progressive nature of this flex in the rod's taper contributes to a smoothness in the release of energy from your casting hand out to the moving fly line.

Most of these popular models lose much of their stiffness somewhere near the middle of the rod, and in this sense are called "medium action" rods. They are thought to provide an attractive balance between power and delicate feel. As you will notice later in the book, there are times when what is termed a "fast" rod, with stiffness farther out into the tip section, may serve your fishing needs. You will also notice that there are times when a "slow" rod, with softness well down into the butt section, is a logical choice.

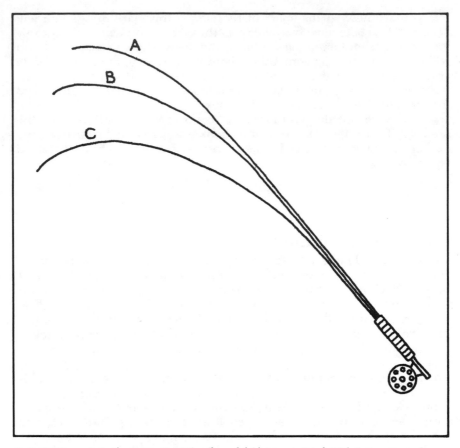

1-1: *Stiffness into the tip section of a fly rod (A) is associated with fast action whereas flexibility into the butt (C) means slow action. Most fly rods are classified as medium action (B).*

If you are interested only in a few of the fly fishing methods described here, or in other fly fishing experiences not covered (e.g., steelhead, shad, striped bass methods), or if you are only 11 years old, your general-purpose fly rod may be somewhat different from the one I have described.

What about reels for fly fishing? For beginning fly fishers, I recommend a moderately-priced, "single action" fly reel (i.e., one complete revolution of the reel's handle rotates the spool one time). The Pflueger Medalist reels have proven to be economical, partly because of their durability. The 1494 and 1494½ models are good trout-size reels. I also enjoy using Martin's MG 7 reel because of its line capacity, lightness, and reasonable price. Yet other anglers, whose opinions I respect, prefer different reels in this price range. Most of these reels have adjustable drag mechanisms, which are adequate for the majority of fishing methods described in this book. They should also be large enough to hold a minimum of 50 yards of small-diameter backing line (e.g., braided nylon or dacron squidding line) in addition to the fly line. This backing provides the extra line you need when a large fish takes your fly more than a hundred feet down stream.

Some fly reels are much more expensive than the models mentioned above. Though machined to fine tolerances, their cost seems out of line with their mechanical simplicity. Some of the expensive reels are fragile, particularly those with an exposed rotating outer rim (used to control drag by pressure of the palm), and become a liability when hit against rocks. (I stumble a lot.) However, well-constructed reels can be important in quiet water when big fish are hooked on fine tippets and move fast enough to overrun a poorly made reel.

1-2: *Author examines a small Hardy, a well-machined, expensive reel that makes sense when fishing for big trout with delicate tippets.*

Though popular a few decades ago, automatic fly reels are heavy, unreliable, and limited in line capacity. I would use one only if I suffered the misfortune of losing one arm.

When it comes to fly lines, I believe it pays to spend the money to buy a quality line—one that lays out smoothly. As of this writing, I am using Cortland (floating) and Scientific Angler (sinking) lines. For a general-purpose first fly line, I recommend a floating, double-tapered (DT), number 6 line to match your rod. The double-tapered line is well suited to the three introductory fishing methods of this book as well as to a number of those that follow. When the enamel inevitably starts to crack on the front taper of your double-tapered line, you can reverse the line on the reel and fish the rear taper. It's like having two fly lines in one.

At the end of your fly line you attach a leader, the length of thin monofilament line that forms the almost invisible link between the fly and the thick easily visible fly line. The tapering down in diameter that begins in the fly line is continued throughout the tapered leader—from its butt at the thick end to its tippet at the small end near the fly. This decrease in the diameter of the line and leader serves to slow the turnover of a cast line and permits your fly to drop gently to the water.

To fish the two most basic fly fishing methods of this book (Chapters 2 and 3), you can purchase a nine-foot knotless leader tapered from .021 inch diameter at the butt down to .007 inch (4X) at the tippet. The nine-foot length is long enough to keep the thick fly line some distance from your fly (and from the fish that approach it) and yet not so long as to make casting difficult.

The 4X or .007 inch diameter indicates how thin the leader tippet is, an important consideration when fishing to leader shy trout. Usually this is a new concept to people who have fished only with bait and lures and are accustomed to thinking of monofilament only in terms of its strength as measured in pounds test. Usually, the smaller diameters are needed in quiet clear water, where fish have the opportunity to inspect the fly carefully. Here a very thin tippet diameter such as .005 inch (6X) may be necessary to draw strikes. However, fish are seldom leader shy in turbulent water where big weighted flies are cast. In this case a thicker tippet diameter such as .010 inch (1X) might be an excellent choice. If the X number is confusing, you can always subtract it from the constant, 11, to obtain the diameter in thousandths of an inch (e.g., 11 - 6X = .005"; 11 - 1X = .010"). This is the so-called "Rule of 11."

One other thing about factory tapered leaders should be mentioned. The last foot or so of the fine end of the leader is not tapered. As long as you cut only this level portion of the leader when changing flies, there is no major problem. However, in a knotless leader there is no obvious way to tell when you have reached and cut into the thicker tapered portion. When this happens your cast fly begins to land on the water heavily. To avoid this problem, you should cut off the last 18 inches of the fine end of your new tapered leader and replace that piece with at least 18 inches of 4X level tippet material. You have made your own leader tippet. Using the leader-to-tippet knot you have just tied as a reference point, you can now see when your tippet becomes too short. If you have changed flies frequently, for example, and have less than 12 inches of tippet left, you have lost much of its strength-giving stretch and should replace it with a new 18- or 24-inch tippet.

Leaders themselves form an esoteric area in the fly fishing world and can become complicatd as you begin to fish different methods on a variety of water types (e.g., riffles, pocket water, glides, still water). Throughout the book I will suggest various leaders that are suited to specific functions (fishing methods).

As you become addicted to fly fishing, you will find yourself beginning to accumulate accessory equipment that is sold in tackle shops. A few bare-bones essentials to start with besides rod, reel and line include fishing license, nail clippers (e.g., "Trim" brand) to cut leader material, a container or fly box to hold extra flies, extra leaders and tippet material, and fly flotant. If you wish to kill fish to eat, you'll need a pocket knife and "arctic" creel. Fishing is often less painful if you carry insect repellent, sun-block cream and dark glasses. Eventually the growing pile of accessories requires the purchase of a vest to hold and organize such items for use.

The flies and wading equipment you decide to use vary with the type of water and the way you fish it. Therefore, they are discussed later in the book.

Assembling the Equipment - Rigging up

The salespeople in many of the better fly fishing shops are trained to attach the backing to the reel, the fly line to the backing, and the leader to the fly line. Where this service is provided, you are able to observe what is involved in putting your line on correctly. This service also simplifies your early preparations at a time when you are being deluged with new terms and concepts. As a result, you may only need to learn two simple knots when first on the stream. On the other hand, if you like to do things for yourself, most of the basic fly fishing handbooks provide adequate detail in rigging up your line and leader.

The knot you will need to use most often on the stream or lake is one to attach your fly to the tippet. I have taught long enough to realize that the most important requirement for a knot used by beginning students is that it be easy to tie. The improved clinch knot combines ease of tying with reasonable strength. Though I often use other knots to attach my fly, I still revert to this one when in a hurry.

The second most necessary knot when fishing is one to connect a new tippet to the leader. Though I use the traditional barrel knot (or blood knot as it is sometimes called) when I want to connect larger diameter segments of a leader neatly or to add a second fly to my leader,

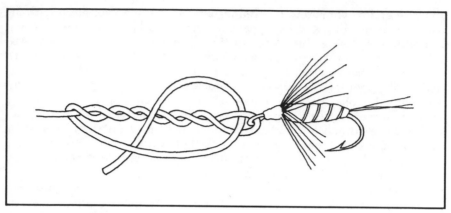

1-3: *Tying the improved clinch knot is easier than it reads:*
1. *Thread the end of the tippet through the eye of the hook,*
2. *wrap this tippet end around the standing part of the leader 5 times and insert it back through the loop in front of the hook eye,*
3. *then bring the end back through the big loop just formed,*
4. *moisten and tighten the knot steadily and trim its tag end.*

I don't recommend it for those beginners who are easily frustrated when knot-tying. It is far simpler to learn the surgeon's knot instead.

Sooner or later you will need to tie a new leader onto your fly line. If you are meticulous by nature, you probably will be drawn to the beauty and neatness of a knot known as the needle knot. However, I prefer the nail knot because it is as reliable as the needle knot and much quicker to tie. Easier yet is the nail-less nail knot, which I use to maintain leaders on the 18 reels I use when teaching. It is also useful when you have to tie a line-leader knot unexpectedly while fishing.

Now you are ready to finish rigging up for casting practice. Plan to practice at least several times before you go fishing. It will make your first experience on the stream far more enjoyable. A good place to practice casting is in the middle of a grass field free of overhead wires with at least 30 feet of space in front of and behind you. If casting pools and instructors are available, so much the better.

Before assembling the fly rod a little paraffin from a candle stub can be applied to the ferrules (where the sections of the fly rod connect). Then you twist (don't twist bamboo) these sections together so the guides for the line are all on the same side of the rod. Attach the reel so that the guides and the reel are on the underside of the rod as it is held out in front of you. The line, coming off the bottom of the reel spool, should feed straight out toward the rod tip.

Whenever you "rig up" on gravel or dirt, and have to set your reel (and rod) down, place your hat on the ground under the reel, to protect it from the grit. Next, strip a couple of yards of line off the reel, fold the

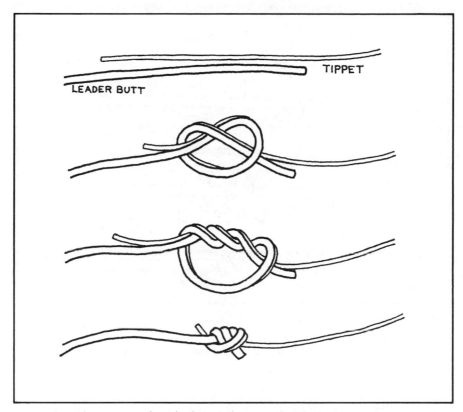

1-4: *Start the surgeon's knot by laying the free end of the leader alongside one end of the tippet so they overlap by 6 to 8 inches. Then each hand holds one end of this doubled strand. The overhand knot is tied with the hand that has the tippet hanging from it. When tippet (and end of leader) have been passed through the loop twice, the knot can be completed by moistening, tightening, and trimming.*

end of the fly line back on itself, and thread it out through the guides. If you push the doubled fly line (rather than the end of the leader) out through the guides, the lines will not slip back down through the guides if accidently let go.

Kinks in the leader can be removed by pulling it between your thumb and forefinger under some pressure (i.e., stretching it). Watch out you don't cut yourself. Finally a tiny tuft of yarn is tied to the end of the tippet to simulate the slight weight and air resistance of the artificial fly. This yarn also stabilizes the end of your tippet, and reduces the likelihood of your being whipped across the face with it. When casting with an actual fly attached, be sure to protect your eyes and the back of your head by wearing glasses and a hat.

1-5: *The "nail-less" nail knot is easier to tie than the standard nail knot but is not quite as neat:*

1. *Start with 8 inches of leader butt alongside the end of the fly line and form a loop in it as illustrated,*
2. *pass the end of the leader butt through the loop 5 or 6 times, progressing away from the end of the fly line,*
3. *pull this leader end to snug the wraps evenly and then tighten the knot,*
4. *trim the ends and smooth the shape of the knot by coating it with flexible cement such as Pliobond or Sally Hansen's* Hard as Nails.

Basic Fly Casting Theory

Casting, or throwing the line, is an important part of many forms of angling. In the popular sport of spin fishing, the weight to be cast is concentrated in a lure, which is propelled through the air like a bullet; thus the lure pulls the line out. Just the opposite is true in fly casting, where the line pulls the lure (fly) out. Here the weight to be cast is distributed throughout a thick fly line, which unrolls on itself when cast, pulling a relatively weightless fly along behind. This difference in mechanics of the two casts is reflected in the way they are executed; the spin cast is a relatively sudden, explosive movement, whereas the fly cast is more prolonged, continuous, and controlled.

This unrolling of line in fly casting places the emphasis on linear characteristics of the movement. The fly line starts extended straight in front of you on the ground (water). In what is termed the "back cast," the line is drawn up and back so that it unrolls until straightened in the air behind the rod tip. Then the line is pulled forward again, unrolled to straighten in the air in front, before being dropped to the practice field (or water) in the forward cast or "forecast." The linear component is evident in that the line straightening behind you is separated by approximately 180 degrees from its straightened position in front of you a second or two later.

To accomplish this straight flow of line, the tip of the fly rod should also be moved in a straight line in much the same plane, at least when power is being applied to pull the line.

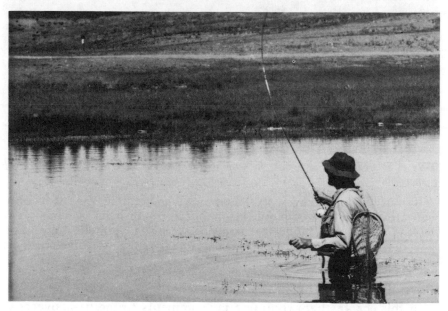

1-6: *Drawing the hand forward in a smooth, continuous manner loads the rod properly.*

This linear movement of the rod tip is achieved by moving your hand along a similar but lower path in a smooth, continuous movement. This movement of the hand transmits power to the line by bending the rod against the resistance of the line. When your hand stops, the power built up by bending or "loading" the rod is released, and the rod straightens and flips the tip over. This "point of turnover" forms a bend or "loop" in the line as it continues forward.

In a well-formed casting loop, the line that extends out from the rod tip is parallel to and beneath the part that is still moving (and hasn't yet turned over). Though it is tempting to see how much line you can cast, your first priority should be to throw well-shaped loops with only 25 to 30 feet of line. You should extend your range only when some measure of loop control has been achieved.

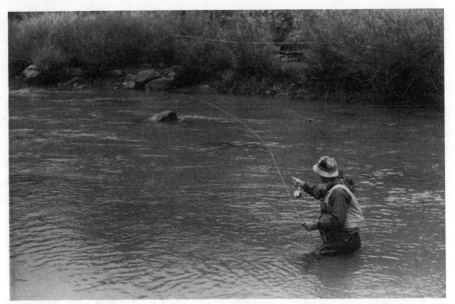

1-7: *A flipped-over rod forms the loop in the fly line and marks the "point of turnover."*

If your line fails to even straighten out when casting, the chances are you are making the common beginner's error of bending your wrist instead of the rod. When this happens your rod tip moves in an arc, which completely disrupts the linear relationships and destroys the cast.

The Basic Overhead Cast

In this chapter I am confining my comments to the basic overhead cast. Other casts may be thought of as variations of the overhead cast, and are introduced later where they apply to particular fishing methods.

Casting is a difficult skill, especially when learning solely from a book. So, I recommend that you seek out a skilled casting instructor and benefit from personal guidance. Frequently such help is available where fly fishing clubs or fly fishing shops exist.

Let's assume that you are back at your practice field, rigged up, and ready to cast. Start with 25 to 30 feet of line beyond the rod tip laid out on the grass in front of you. Grip the rod handle so that your thumb is nearly parallel to the grip and is placed somewhere near the top—comfort is important. Use only your casting or "rod hand" for now by trapping the line under the first or second finger. The use of the non-casting or "line hand" is best introduced later, when you have had time to concentrate on what the rod and rod hand should be doing. An improperly used line hand can detract from what the feel of the rod should be.

In executing the pick-up and lay-down or water cast, you pick-up or lift the line off the grass (water) with your backcast, pausing for the line to straighten behind you. Then you make the forward cast, which lays the line down on the grass again in front. The numbers below correspond to those in the accompanying illustrations, which are based on tracings of high speed photographs of a fly rod's movement.

The Backcast

1. Start low. At the start of the back cast the rod tip is held low, so it will begin to bend or load as early as possible. If you load the rod late, by starting off with a high tip, you may feel the need to continue the stroke too far in back, which drops the line too low behind you.

2. Move the Line. As you begin to move the line toward you on the grass by moving the rod butt upward and back, the rod begins to load in the flexible tip section.

1-8: *The Backcast*

3. Speed up. As your hand begins to move faster, the rod loads farther down into the butt section. In a long cast, the flex would be more pronounced than that shown in the drawing. Excessive wrist action at this time can throw the rod tip back early and drop the line low behind you.

4. Stop. As the flex of the rod starts rolling back out toward the tip, the hand stops the rod butt. It is often helpful to combine the cues, "Speed up and Stop," as Lefty Kreh does in his teaching. Where this acceleration and stop occurs sets the direction for the continued backward movement of the line. A friend can be of great help to you by watching your backcast from the side and telling you the direction the line is moving back, whether it is straightening, and what the loop looks like (i.e., shape, size).

5. If the rod has been loaded and stopped as described, it should bend back rather than downward after straightening.

6. Drift. Once the rod has been stopped, you can loosen your wrist and tip the rod back a little without causing the line to drop. This backward "drift" positions the rod for full loading of the forward cast.

The Forecast

7. Pause. It is usually necessary to pause briefly at the completion of the drift to allow the line to straighten behind you before starting the forward cast. How long you pause depends on how much line is being straightened; additional line requires extra time.

8. Pull the butt. When the line has almost straightened to the rear, you begin the forward cast by moving your hand so as to pull your rod butt forward. The flex, which starts again in the tip, progresses down into the butt under increased loading. This hand movement should be

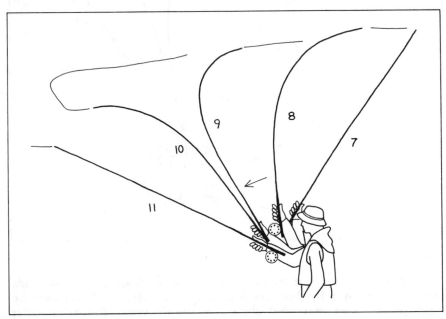

1-9: *The Forward Cast or Forecast*

smooth and continuous, because the line has started moving forward and its flow shouldn't be disrupted by a jerky or uneven thrust.

9. Put a loop in the rod. Mel Krieger's phrase catches the essence of what should happen during this critical part of the cast. The flex, or loop, progresses up the rod and rolls off the tip. Try to feel this bend in your rod progress outward from your hand during the forward cast; if you watch your rod, you can see it happening before the stop. This is an important concept to work with if your line tends to cross itself in what is called a tailing loop.

10. Stop. When you stop the forward cast, the rod straightens and flips over. If you have loaded it progressively, this reverse deflection of the rod should be outward as shown, rather than downward. Thus the shock is absorbed into the butt rather than in a downward-dipping tip.

Where the tip stops is where the bottom of the casting loop forms in the line. So the higher the stop, the smaller the depth of the loop.

11. Follow down. As the last of the line unrolls forward, you continue to lower the rod to achieve a gentle drop of the fly to the grass (water).

Throughout this discussion I have emphasized the progressive nature of the loading of a fly rod. I have done so because I think it is an important concept that has not received enough attention in the casting literature.

I think we sometimes get sidetracked by relatively unimportant differences of style in casting techniques. Some of us differ in recommended stances, grips, hand and elbow positions, and use of the wrist. Even our most respected casting instructors—people like Mel Krieger, Joan Wulff, Lefty Kreh, Harry Wilson, and Chris Korich—have different casting and teaching styles. However, the important thing is that they all succeed in getting their students to bend the rod properly so that line will lay out smoothly. That is what fly casting is all about.

False Casting

The false cast is so named because the line isn't allowed to drop to the water to be fished; in this sense it's not the real thing. False casts are used to work out additional line, measure the amount of line in relation to your target, change the direction of your cast, and dry off your fly. False casting should be practiced as should the pick-up and lay-down, because both are used in fishing and both require different casting planes. Because the false cast starts with the line in the air in front of you (rather than on the ground), there isn't as much opportunity to lift the line in back. Therefore the casting plane is more horizontal.

Adding the Line Hand

Though we have been casting with the "rod hand" only, you probably are aware that the line is held in the non-casting or "line hand" when casting to catch fish. When you first add the line hand to your practice casting, you should hold it down near your stomach to make sure the line is anchored away from the rod. If this is not done and your line hand moves up near the rod, you may be feeding line into the cast and interfering with the loading of the rod.

When you learn to double haul with the line hand (as introduced in Chapter 6), you will know how to tighten the line with little tugs during both the backcast and the forecast.

The Trout and its Environment

There is more to fishing than equipment and casting. This becomes evident when you watch beginning anglers casting about indiscriminately as if the trout must be everywhere. Most of us learn from experience that trout are not randomly or evenly distributed in a lake or stream. In order to have an idea of where to fish, you need to know something about trout and its aquatic environment. Some of this basic information is presented here because it holds true regardless of the fishing method you use.

First of all, trout are found in cold water. They are thought to be able to survive in water between 40 and 80 degrees F., but usually feed within a more restricted range. Joe Humphreys, a knowledgeable Eastern fly fisher and teacher, has recently stated that the closer the temperature is to 61 degrees F., the more frequent rainbow and brown trout feed. In his book, *Joe Humphrey's Trout Tactics*, he builds a strong case for the importance of water temperature and the use of a water thermometer.

The content of oxygen in water also determines where fish may hold. In well-aerated water, the supply of oxygen is seldom a problem for trout, but high temperature, acidity, excessive weed-growth, and pollution can all work to deplete oxygen supply. When this happens, for example, as a result of hot summer weather, trout may be forced to move to the most aerated riffles.

Usually, however, trout are found where they are safe from predators. This safety comes from the overhead cover afforded by large rocks, logs, weed beds, deep water, undercut banks, or riffled water. In *The Ecology of Running Waters*, Hynes characterizes mountain streams as alternating deep and shallow areas—deep basins and riffles. The depth of the basins, the choppy surface of the riffles, and any large mid-stream rocks provide much of the trout's cover. Hynes characterizes meadow streams by the meandering nature of their channels, which have a "regularity of curving pattern, regardless of stream size." Wherever the main current intersects a bank, it has the potential to erode out a deep, undercut area. Trout use these areas and mid-stream weed beds for cover in this type of water.

Even when trout feed in the shallows, they are seldom far from the protection of deeper water. In lakes, for example, they frequently cruise the shoreline close to where it drops off sharply. The food is generally abundant in the shallow areas where water plants thrive, but protection is found in deep water beyond the drop off.

A trout's safety is enhanced by its well-developed sensory organs. With independent, protruding eyes on each side of its head—eyes that can move in their sockets—a trout can see in all directions, with the exception of the 30 degrees directly behind it. These fish can also detect vibrations and pressure differences in the water in excess of 50 feet under quiet conditions. Therefore you may need to keep low, tread quietly, avoid loud colors in your clothing, and generally stalk or hunt your fish.

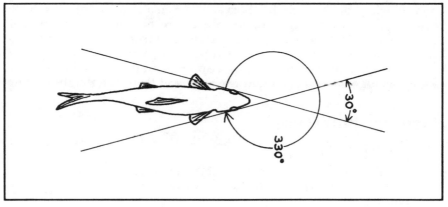

1-10: *The sight-gifted trout's only blind spot is directly in back. This vision is important to predation as well as protection, because the trout is a sight hunter.*

Specific information on "reading the water," or studying it to determine where trout should be holding, is available in many books. Charles Brook's *The Trout and the Stream* and *Larger Trout for the Western Angler* remain two of my favorites. Gary Borger has a well-organized chapter on trout lies in *Nymphing,* in which he seems to build on material developed by Hynes. What I do in the following chapters of this book is to describe specific water types as part of "The Fishing Situation" that sets the stage for each method of fishing.

Where trout are found is frequently where food is available. In streams, trout face upcurrent and see food that drifts downstream toward them. Sometimes they feed without moving from their protected "lies." Other times they must leave this "holding water" to find food, either by foraging along the bottom or stationing themselves in nearby "feeding water" where drifting food is concentrated. As indicated previously, trout in lakes frequently cruise along the shoreline to find food.

Most pan-sized trout feed on insects, both land-born (terrestrial) and aquatic. Land insects such as ants, beetles, leafhoppers, and grasshoppers sometimes get blown into the water and drift downstream. Aquatic insects that you might know by their common names— mayflies, caddisflies, stoneflies, dragonflies, damselflies, midges—are eaten under water in immature nymph, larva or pupa stages and on the surface as they emerge into winged flies or alight later to lay eggs.

The artificial flies you use when fishing are typically tied to resemble such insects either generally or specifically—in terms of size, shape, color, and even texture. Chapters 3 and 4 of Charles Brook's *Nymph Fishing for Larger Trout* provide an excellent introduction to insect life in the water. If you are looking for a first general book on what I would term angler's entomology, I recommend either *Western Hatches* by Hafele and Hughes or *Naturals* by Borger. The main focus of this book, however, is on learning fish, so insects are mentioned only in their obvious associations with particular fly patterns, aquatic habitat, or fishing methods.

By now you must be ready to move on to the business of fishing. You know enough about equipment, casting, and trout for the time being.

General References

Anderson, S. *The Curtis Creek Manifesto.* Portland Oregon: Salmon Trout Steelheader, 1976.

Brooks, J. *Trout Fishing.* New York: Harper & Row, 1972.

Scientific Anglers. *Fly Fishing Handbook.* 1st. Ed. Midland, Michigan: Scientific Anglers, 1977.

Scientific Anglers. *Fly Fishing Made Easy.* Point Pleasant, New Jersey: Aqua-Field, 1981.

Basic Casting References

Green, J. *Fly Casting...from the Beginning.* Westminster, Ca: Fenwick/- Sevenstrand, 1971.

Krieger, M. "Understanding the Casting Arc," *Fly Fisherman,* 1979, Early Season.

References on the Trout and its Environment

Borger, G. *Naturals.* Harrisburg, Pa.: Stackpole, 1979.

Borger, G. *Nymphing—A Basic Book.* Harrisburg, Pa.: Stackpole, 1979.

Brooks, C.E. *Larger Trout for the Western Flyfisherman.* New York: A.S. Barnes, 1970.

Brooks, C.E. *Nymph Fishing for Larger Trout.* New York: Crown, 1976.

Brooks, C.E. *The Trout and the Stream.* New York: Crown, 1974.

Hafele, R. and Hughes, D. *The Complete Book of Western Hatches.* Portland: Frank Amato, 1981.

Humphreys, J. *Joe Humphrey's Trout Tactics.* Harrisburg, Pa.: Stackpole, 1981.

Hynes, H.B.N. *The Ecology of Running Water.* Toronto: University of Toronto Press, 1970.
Needham, P.R. *Trout Streams.* New York: Winchester, 1969.

Other References
Helleckson, T. *Popular Fly Patterns.* Salt Lake City: Peregrine Smith, 1977.
Kreh, L. and Sosin, M. *Practical Fishing Knots.* New York: Crown, 1972.
Leiser, E. *The Complete Book of Fly Tying.* New York: Alfred A. Knopf, 1978.

2
THE DOWN AND ACROSS SWING
A Basic Wet Fly Method For Streams

The Fishing Situation

A wide riffle is an ideal type of water in which to learn the basic down and across wet fly method. The riffle should be wide enough to permit a 20 to 30 foot cast directly across stream. The choppy, riffling nature of the water's surface helps to conceal you from the trout, minimizing the need for a quiet approach and splash-free cast. The wading, which can be traumatic to some beginners, is seldom difficult in shallow, gravel-bottomed riffles. Even the across-stream cast simplifies learning by presenting the fly on a line that is tightening as it moves downstream away from you. This tight line enables you to experience some early success by hooking trout that wouldn't be felt or caught on a slack line.

Riffles have another important feature. They harbor a wide variety of small animals that trout eat. The gravel and larger rocks on the bottom provide cover for small, immature insects such as mayfly nymphs and caddis larva as well as larger predators that seek them out, including stonefly nymphs, dragonfly nymphs, small fish (e.g., sculpin), and crayfish. Trout frequently use riffles as "feeding water."

Rigging Adaptations

The basic, general-purpose fly fishing equipment described in the first chapter will serve you well in fishing these riffles. A useful consideration when initially faced with the problem of selecting a fly is to obtain a few weighted patterns that represent a wide variety of the insect life that trout feed on. A popular, readily-available wet fly or nymph that does this is the Gold-Ribbed Hare's Ear nymph; it loosely resembles several common forms of aquatic life, including some mayfly nymphs, caddisfly larva and caddisfly pupa. Tied in a size 10 or 12 with about 6 turns of 2-amp lead-fuse wire under the body material, this fly

2-1: *Impressionistic nymphs such as a Gold-Ribbed Hare's Ear resemble a variety of immature aquatic insects.*

is large enough to attract the trout's attention in choppy water and heavy enough to reach many of the bottom currents where trout most often lie. Where the water is less turbulent, a smaller, less-weighted size 14 Hare's Ear is better.

A 9-foot leader, tapered down to 4X is a good starting point for fishing the wide riffles associated with this basic method.

The Approach

Before you start to fish, why not sample the stream bottom for insects. Find out which insects are abundant in that section of stream. When you learn to recognize various types of aquatic insects, you begin to understand why certain artificial flies look the way they do. You begin to know when to use particular fly patterns.

An effective screen for collecting insects can be made by stapling a piece of window screen (i.e., 2 feet high by 3 feet across) between two poles or sticks (e.g., old broom sticks). The bottom of the screen should be almost flush with the bottom of the poles to prevent insects from escaping underneath. At the stream, you place the screen downstream of a likely-looking rock and hold it there while you lift up the rock. Insects that swim or drift away are swept into your screen, while those that cling to the rock can be picked off by hand. This collecting should not disturb the exact water you will be fishing.

The most common error in insect collecting is to sample from one aquatic habitat only. Be sure to sample from slow as well as fast currents, from sand and gravel as well as rubble bottom, and from submerged sticks and aquatic vegetation as well as rocks.

I have indicated that the water selected for this method of fly fishing is wide enough and turbulent enough to permit you to use an across-stream cast without spooking fish. Because it's not always apparent where fish are lying in a riffle, nor how many fish are feeding there, you should cover such water systematically. The most common aproach is to wade in at the head of the riffle (upstream end). Your first casts are made from the shore at times. You fish the near water with a short line, then when the line has been extended, you cover the water farther out. Next, you move a few steps downstream and repeat this near-to-far sequence. This procedure is repeated until the riffle has been fished from head to tail.

In many streams your success will depend on the time of day you select to fish. This point was brought home to me vividly one June evening some years ago. My friend Dick Holland and I drove all day and weren't able to start fishing till 7:30 pm. I had the only car key and didn't want Dick to have to wait for me, so I quit fishing at nine o'clock. It turns out we had each caught three modest-sized trout by that time. But while I walked back to the car, Dick continued to fish. In the extra half-hour, he hooked four more fish—all substantially larger than those we caught from the same water before 9:00 pm.

2-2: *Dropping to one knee provides concealment for the first, short casts at the head of a riffle.*

A week later I checked this time-of-day effect on a heavily-fished riffle of a fairly small stream. I had watched several anglers fish it that day and take a total of two rainbow trout between 6 and 8 inches long. That evening, on my first cast, I caught a 15-inch brown trout. Brown trout are known to adapt particularly well to the presence of anglers by feeding at night. And that riffle had a large log off to one side, which provided an excellent daytime hold for a decent fish. It's always a good idea when approaching a riffle to make note of obvious cover. Then, if it's feasible, return to fish the riffle again on the way back to your car. You may be pleasantly surprised.

When fishing big rivers I constantly keep an eye out for shallow, wide riffles off to one side of deep heavy runs. Some of these riffles are wide and long enought to cover an extensive area of stream bottom. And this type of bottom is ideally suited to many species of aquatic insects. On a summer evening thousands of insects may emerge from a single riffle. The deep, heavy water off to the side provides daytime cover for large trout—often a surprising number of large trout. Under the cover of dusk, these trout sometimes move into the shallow riffles to feed voraciously while expending very little energy. When insects are emerging in large numbers, this may be the trout's only feeding time.

Casting Techniques

All that is required of you as a beginning angler in this method is to be able to cast a fly line a distance of up to 30 feet. This includes the ability to false cast as a means of extending the line as well as estimating the amount needed to reach your chosen spot.

Line-Handling and Fishing Techniques

Immediately after the cast, the line being held in your line hand should be brought over to your rod hand and hooked in the index or second finger of that hand (the finger used is a matter of personal preference). This finger of the rod hand becomes the point at which you maintain control of the drifting line. Then any retrieving of line can be done most easily by the line hand's pulling in or "stripping in" line a few inches at a time from behind this control point.

2-3: *Stripping in line begins by grasping it just behind and below where it is controlled by the rod hand.*

After the cast has been made the line and fly drift downstream. Should part of the line get downstream ahead of the fly, it creates a curve or belly on the water that begins to pull the fly across stream unnaturally fast, thus disrupting a natural drift. When this happens, you should lift some of the fly line off the water and place it down again in a different alignment, most often a little farther upstream. This line-handling technique, the upstream mend, is accomplished by lifting the

2-4: *The line is stripped or pulled down a few inches. It is then released to fall toward the water as the line hand returns upward to make the next strip.*

2-5: *Mending line involves lifting the floating part off the water and placing it down again off to whichever side affords an improved drift.*

rod tip and moving it upstream whenever the drifting line starts to overtake the fly. The line may have to be mended several times during the same drift. With proper mending, the entire drifting portion of the fly line remains a little upstream of the fly, which allows it to sink and drift downstream naturally.

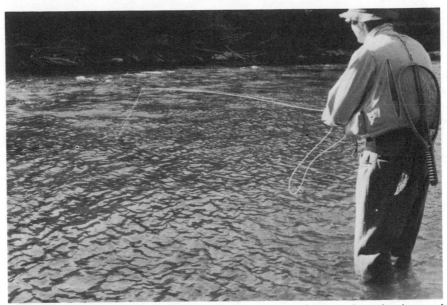

2-6: *Fishing the drift with line moving downstream from left to right and rod pointed toward the fly.*

2-7: *Mending or lifting the floating line off the water is done to reposition it in better alignment with the fly. Here the line will be replaced farther upstream.*

As soon as the line is mended, you should return the tip of the fly rod to a low position over the water and point it at the drifting fly throughout the remainder of its drift. Continue to point the rod tip at the fly during the swing across the current after the line tightens, and the retrieve back upstream toward you.

A retrieve may not be necessary on very short casts, but on long casts it is a convenient means of recovering enough line to be able to lift it off the water effortlessly for the next false cast. Sometimes fish that have ignored your drifting fly will strike as it is being actively retrieved upstream. As previously indicated, the simplest and most common way to retrieve line is to strip it in with the line hand from behind the rod hand. As the line comes in, hold it in loose loops or just let it fall on the water.

Hooking and Landing the Fish

There are different schools of thought on how to set the hook when a trout takes your fly. To some extent these different techniques depend on the fly fishing method and water type being fished. This will become more apparent as you read some of the chapters that follow.

As a beginning fly fisher you may find youself so preoccupied with casting, knot-tying and line-handling that you fail to give much thought to how the hook should be set. If the hook is set at all on your first few fish, it is probably a natural-tendency technique of lifting the hand, arm and fly rod, often with excessive force. Lifting the fly rod continues to serve you well in some methods, though many experienced fly fishers begin to rely increasingly on the line hand to do at least part of this job.

The whole idea in setting the hook is to tighten the line and move the fly enough to allow penetration of the hook into the trout's jaw. The more slack line that is on the water, the more pronounced your movements of rod tip and/or line hand must be to achieve this tightening. There is a fine line between too much and too little force to set the hook. This comes with experience.

Once the fish has been hooked, the most important thing at this level of angling is to keep the line tight. Should the fish move toward you, this tightness can be maintained by stripping line in as discussed in the previous section on retrieving. If wading, you can slowly and carefully wade back to shore, leading the fish in that direction while it is still underwater. When close to shore, you can quickly lift the fish out and swing it far enough overland to prevent it from flopping back into the water should the hook come loose.

If the fish is small and you want to release it, you can bring it directly in to you at midstream. At times you will be able to release it by touching only the hook—turning it so the point of the hook is down. When you do this, trout sometimes fall off the hook as a result of their own movements. Surgical hemostats may be carried to remove deeply imbedded hooks. However you release fish, handle them gently without squeezing and place them in the water facing upstream. Watch to make sure the gills are functioning properly. Gradually loosen your hold to check whether or not a trout can maintain an upright, balanced position in the water. When it has recovered, the fish should be able to swim out of your hold.

2-8: *Watching a healthy trout swim away and knowing you haven't depleted a fishery brings satisfaction.*

Such catch-and-release fishing is the best single management tool we have to assure a continued supply of healthy, wild trout. It is best done with barbless hooks, or hooks that have had the barb pressed flat to contribute to a higher survival rate. Most anglers expect to lose their fish when first switching to barbless hooks, and it is amusing to see their reaction when this doesn't happen. If you are like most of us, you will feel sheepish about not having switched sooner. The trend is to fish barbless.

Wading and Safety

In guiding classes of beginning anglers, I have found that many people who are unaccustomed to walking in trout streams become quite anxious about their safety. Actually feeling the current against their legs does little to reassure them, and often distracts them from the attention needed in learning to fish. Consequently, I prefer to give my basic fly fishing instruction where currents don't move fast enough to be disconcerting and under sunny conditions, when the stream bottom is clearly visible.

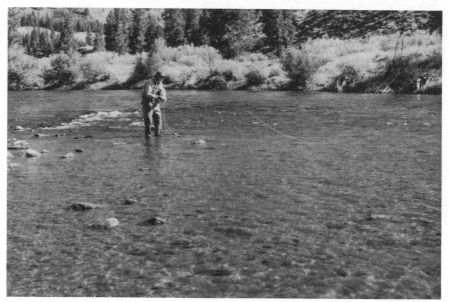

2-9: *Sunny weather and shallow riffles reduce anxious feelings about wading.*

An additional advantage of selecting the warm part of the day to fish is evident if you are unable to purchase hip or chest waders. The warm conditions enable you to "wade wet" in relative comfort. You may find you prefer to wade in wet jeans when temperatures permit. However, you should be aware that it could lead to hypothermia if practiced in cold conditions or if you delay changing out of your wet clothes after fishing.

If there is a cardinal rule of safety while wading it is to wade well within your limits. These limits can be extended through experience or through the assistance of a good instructor.

Riffles are generally safe places to wade. In them you typically fish from the shallow, gently-sloping side of the stream where relatively small, gravel-sized rocks have been deposited. However, movements toward deeper water may lead you to areas where the stream bottom slopes more abruptly. Here some danger exists because gravel on a slope can move underfoot and create a ball-bearing-effect that can slide you to a dunking in deep water.

Variations of this Method

The down-stream drift and across-stream swing of a fly forms the basis for several other, more specific and demanding fly fishing methods. For example, by casting a longer line, developing distinctive retrieves, and roll casting a sinking line to the surface, you have the essentials of big river streamer (i.e., a fly that imitates a bait fish) fishing and steelhead fishing. E.H. "Polly" Rosborough, the highly regarded nymph tyer and angler, has found a down-and-across approach well suited to his shallow nymph and streamer techniques on the wide, moderately paced rivers he fishes in southern Oregon.

Selected References

Borger, G. "Invertebrate Drift," *Rod and Reel,* 1979, July/August.

Hidy, V. *Sports Illustrated Book of Wet-Fly Fishing.* Philadelphia: J.B. Lippencott, 1961.

Leisenring, J. and Hidy, V. *The Art of Tying the Wet Fly and Fishing the Nymph* New York: Crown, 1971.

Nemes, S. *The Soft Hackled Fly.* Old Greenwich, Ct: Chatham, 1975.

Rosborough, E.H. *Tying and Fishing the Fuzzy Nymphs.* Caldwell, Idaho: Caxton, 1965, Harrisburg, Pa: Stackpole, 1978.

3
DRY FLY FISHING IN MOUNTAIN LAKES
A Basic Lake Method

The Fishing Situation

If you are ready to learn dry (floating) fly fishing, try to locate a lake where trout feed hungrily on the surface. Many alpine lakes are ideal for learning this method because their unusually short growing season and sterile water force trout to feed almost constantly, inhaling anything that swims, crawls, or flies too close. Often one or two trout will cruise in a long straight line just off shore trying to obtain enough food to survive.

This cruising behavior illustrates a basic distinction between lake-dwelling and stream-dwelling trout. Trout in lakes most often cruise or move to find food, whereas trout in streams tend to hold in or move to feeding stations and take food carried within reach by the current.

Dry fly fishing is easier to learn in a mountain lake than in a stream because the line handling in the lake method is simpler. When keeping your fly visible, looking for fish, and setting the hook, without also having to strip line in frantically to keep pace with a current.

Rigging Adaptations

Our general-purpose fly rod and line are well suited to this method of fly fishing, though lake anglers don't always agree on the type of

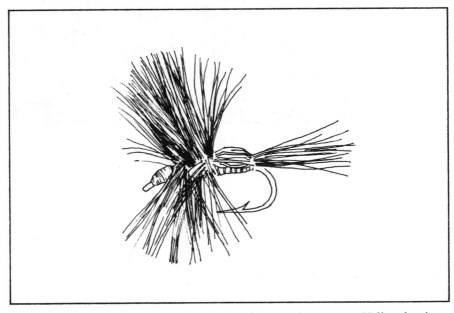

3-1: *This heavily-dressed Humpy has been tied for rough-water use. Hollow deer hair, excessive hackle, and unusually long hackle and tail all suggest a concern for flotation rather than for tying proportions.*

floating line to use. If you fish where trees or high rock ledges prevent a backcast, you will need the roll-casting (discussed in this chapter) capability of a double-tapered line. However, if obstacles to casting are not a problem and you are experienced in casting with a double haul (discussed in Chapter 6), you wil most likely prefer the distance advantages of a weight-forward line.

Fish are often spooky in clear lake water, so our 9-foot leader may need to be lengthened to 12 feet at times. Under these conditions you may want to switch from a general-purpose "attractor" dry fly, such as a size 12 Humpy, to a smaller and more delicate pattern, such as a size 14 or 16 Adams. While the Humpy is constructed to float on more turbulent water than the Adams, both are superb general-purpose flies: Both are tied with mixed brown and grizzly hackle (i.e., the feather wrapped around the hook to represent the legs and sometimes the wings of an insect) and are medium-toned to cover the widest spectrum of colors typically seen in aquatic insects. Also both patterns have general insect shapes that take fish when either caddisflies or mayflies are on the water or when nothing at all is on the water.

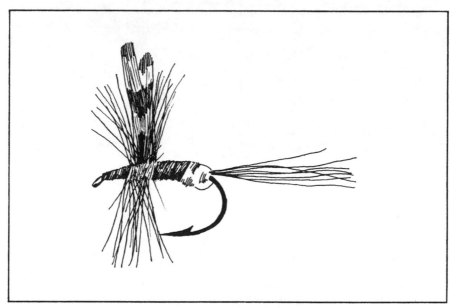

3-2: *The ever-present Adams is our most popular "standard dry fly" for quiet water. The light body color near the tail of this one represents a mayfly's egg sac.*

I recall a few moments on Lake Solitude in Grand Teton National Park when this basic mountain-lake rigging served me well. The 15-mile round-trip hike was taking longer than my wife, Barbara, and I had anticipated, so we had agreed to stop at the lake only long enough to eat lunch. But, coming up the trail I had assembled my rod and attached a size 14 Adams to the 9-foot leader (back-packing anglers learn to assemble equipment on the move). As I ate, the rod was at my side with 35 feet of line on the ground beyond the rod tip. No one we had met on the trail that day had seen a fish rise, but as luck would have it, one came up while I was eating—within casting range. I laid down my sandwich, picked up the fly rod, and caught a 14-inch cutthroat on one cast, without even getting up. Trout are seldom so accommodating.

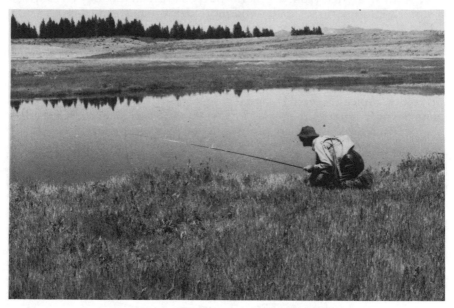

3-3: *Keep low to avoid being seen by cruising trout in transparent water.*

The Approach

Perhaps the most fundamental principle in approaching a trout lake or stream is that the quieter and clearer the water, the more careful and stealthy your approach. Thus in clear alpine lakes, it may be necessary to use a tree or a rock as a "blind" and then to cast the fly well ahead of any visible fish so it will not be spooked by the cast. More typically, however, you will try to analyze the pattern of rises (i.e., the trout's surface feeding). If a cruising fish rises frequently, you learn to wait for its second rise to determine the direction the trout is moving, and then place the fly ahead of it. When rises are isolated and fish are not too spooky, you cast directly to the spot of the rise. To get it there soon enough, you may have to be false casting so that your line is already in the air when a promising rise appears.

3-4: *Casting beyond the second rise is based on the trout's tendency to cruise in a relatively straight line.*

At times the fish in such lakes are not rising but may still be taken on a dry fly. Under these conditions, you should be playing the percentages in locating fish rather than casting randomly along some shoreline. Move to a spot where you believe fish are likely to be found. One such spot would be the outlet of a lake, where the subtle currents of the lake converge and carry surface-born food from a wide area into the same spot. Another high-percentage spot for locating trout is near the inlet where fresh, oxygenated water and some food enter the lake. Fishing near aquatic vegetation is worthwhile because it provides cover for trout as well as cover and food for the aquatic animals trout feed on. Partially submerged rocks or logs near shore also provide shaded cover in the vicinity of land insects, such as ants and beetles, that are frequently blown into lakes.

Casting Techniques

In dry fly fishing, the false cast helps to dry your fly off for the next presentation. Casting is normally done with the basic overhead cast, though the roll cast becomes an important tool on lakes where trees crowd the shoreline and prevent backcasting.

The roll cast starts when the line has been slowly drawn back toward you on the water and the rod tip is back just past vertical. The elbow of your casting arm may be at least as high as your shoulder at the start of the forward stroke to provide more distance through which your hand

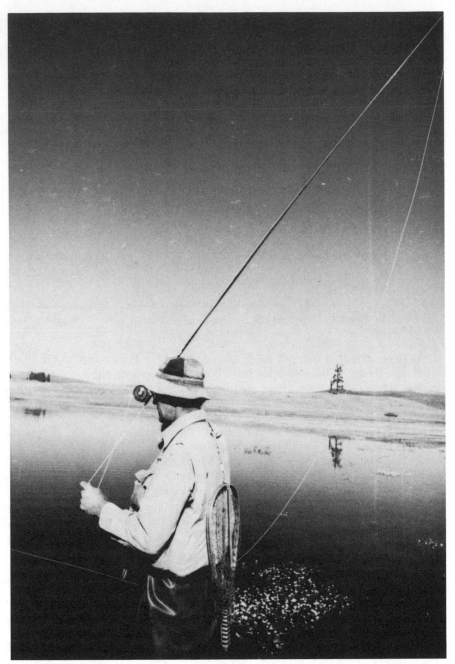

3-5: *In the roll cast you draw the line back on the water rather than cast it back in the air.*

can move down in applying power. The maximum acceleration comes when the rod tip is forward enough to provide a low, knifing oval in the line's roll-out. The "circle shaped" roll sometimes pictured doesn't have the same distance potential and usually results from applying power too early in the cast. This is an important teaching point in Mel Krieger's instruction.

3-6 *The forward thrust of the roll cast lifts line off the water and returns it to the water beyond the rod tip. Though this "roll of line" is not visible against the light sky, it progresses out from the angler until the fly is lifted from the water and rolled farther out.*

Several variations of the basic cast are useful in lake fly fishing. The ability to "shoot line" enables you to add distance to your cast. To do this, simply strip extra line off the reel and let it slip through the fingers of your line hand (and out through the guides of your rod) on the forward cast.

Wind often comes up on lakes and so you may have to make adjustments in the basic cast. To use a wind from behind to your advantage, you lower the angle of your backcast and raise that of your forward cast; in this way the wind carries your fly farther. A wind into your face can be overcome by raising your backcast and lowering the forecast to get a low, hard-driving layout of line. A wind from the side of your casting arm leads you to cast the rod overhead so the rod tip, fly line, and fly move back and forth on your non-casting side. This technique of casting-off-the-left-shoulder is described as the off-side cast in Chapter 10.

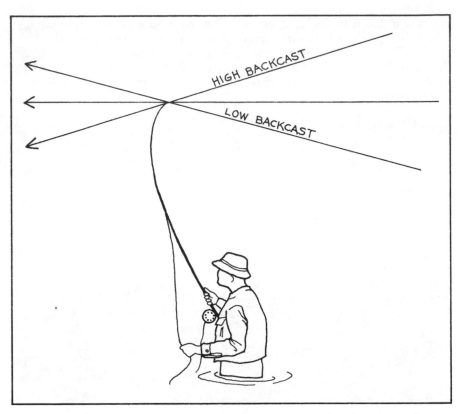

3-7: *Casting from low-backcast to high-forecast carries the fly when the wind comes from behind. High-backcast to low-forecast drives the fly line into a wind that blows into your face.*

Line-Handling and Fishing Techniques

In most dry fly fishing in lakes, you permit the fly to drift naturally on the surface without being twitched. The only line-handling is an occasional stripping-in of slack that forms as a result of wave action. This line-handling is much easier than that needed to continually keep pace with the currents of most streams.

A trout that is approaching your fly should not be able to see you. Crouching and keeping a low silhouette will help. But when your fly begins to drift close enough for fish and fisherman to see each other, the fly should be lifted gently off the water and recast to a spot farther away. If no fish are rising, you may want to cover the water system-atically by casting to various angles with a relatively short cast and then "fanning" across again with longer casts. This is nothing more than a lake variation of the near-to-far concept.

Hooking and Landing the Fish

Seeing the fish take your fly provides the excitement that keeps some people fishing dry flies exclusively throughout their lives. Most anglers set the hook in this method by gently lifting the rod enough to take up whatever slack has formed in the line on the water.

Wading and Safety

Some backpackers who fly fish the high mountain lakes leave their waders at home. They find it difficult to justify space for such a large item. Instead of wading, they often fish when the trout have moved in toward shore—during morning and evening hours.

Other backpackers don extra pants and tennis shoes, choosing to wade wet. Care must be taken to respect the danger of hypothermia from the combination of cold lake water and fast-cooling afternoons.

Among the most dedicated flyfishing/backpackers, are a group who insist on taking along a pair of modern, light-weight, stocking-foot waders to use with tennis shoes. A few even pack in light-weight inflatable float-tubes to cover all the water.

Variations of this Method

The trout in lakes often become selective in their surface feeding, which leads you into the world of "matching the hatch"; that is, obtaining fly patterns that are specific imitations of the insects fish are feeding on (discussed in Chapter 12). Mayflies and midges are two common sources of this selective feeding.

At times you will find that a naturally-drifting fly isn't as effective in attracting trout as one that is actively manipulated. On such occasions you intentionally create motion by twitching, skittering or crawling your fly to excite the trout. If you see ants struggling in the surface film, caddisflies paddling toward shore while emerging, or winged adults skittering along the surface while depositing their eggs, you have a behavior to imitate when retrieving your fly.

Sometimes trout feed on insects floating or moving just under the surface. You should consider this possibility when only the trout's back breaks the surface during its rise. When you see this, change your fly to something such as an unweighted nymph or a spinner (i.e., dying adult mayfly) pattern fished flush in the surface film or slightly submerged.

Selected References

Almy, G. "What Makes a Good Dry Fly," *The Flyfisher*, 1981, Winter.

Mitchell, R. "Recommendation for an Alpine Idyll," *Angler*, 1981, Early Spring.

Rajeff, S. "Casting with Steve Rajeff—The Roll Cast," *Angler*, January-February, 1977.

Raymond, S. "Still Water-Ponds and Lakes," in J. Migel (Ed.), *The Masters on The Dry Fly*, Philadelphia: Lippencott, 1977.

Roberts, D. "Lakes: Scratching the Surface," *Flyfishing the West*, 1978, March-April.

4
SHORT-LINE,
DRY FLY FISHING
An Introduction To
Upstream Fly Fishing

The Fishing Situation

The water type that is most appropriate to the method discussed here is "pocket water"—short pools of slow water found among the faster currents of mountain streams. These short pools may be formed by large rocks, logs, or other obstacles that deflect the stream's currents, either at midstream or along a bank. Such "pocket water" is typical of the steeper sections of small mountain streams or of the cascading runs of large streams. When a big midstream rock diverts current flow, it creates small areas of slower-moving water that provide a mini-environment where aquatic plants flourish, slow-water insects colonize, and trout hold without expending much energy. For dry fly fishing, shallow pockets are generally best because bottom-holding trout will often move the two or three feet to reach the surface; the deeper the pocket water, the less the bigger fish are likely to rise to feed on top.

Dry flies work well throughout long periods of the day in many creeks. This is partly because food is seldom abundant there, and trout become accustomed to rising to any terrestrial insects that happen to fall onto the water. In narrow creeks it is not unrealistic to think of trout as the ultimate "bank feeders," because both banks contribute food to the same fish. In alpine creeks the winter kill of insects and the sterility of water add to a trout's survival problems and lead to almost continual feeding.

The problems you face in fishing pocket water are largely a result of the short length of pools or the extreme variation in current speed. In order to drift your fly slowly through short pools, you must be able to move in close enough to the fish to keep line from falling on fast currents. Also you must be able to keep your fly from being dragged along the surface by currents moving at different speeds. Additionally you must learn to prevent excessive slack from developing in your upstream-cast line.

Rigging Adaptations

Our basic fly rod, reel, and line will work well in pocket water, though many anglers who fish regularly in such water prefer a rod action on the soft side of medium; they want flex down toward the butt of the rod so it will bend enough to present a fly with delicacy when only a few feet of fly line extend beyond the rod tip. Stiffness in a rod butt often makes an important, positive contribution to loop control where long casts are used, but it interferes with the feel I prefer when casting a short-line in pocket water.

Also related to these short casts is the use of short leaders, typically from 6 to 7½ feet in length. Short leaders enable you to let out a little additional line beyond the rod tip to load the rod when casting at close range. It is easier to cast line than leader.

Most pocket-water dry fly anglers have one or two favorite general-purpose fly patterns, usually in sizes 10 or 12. The moderate degree of surface turbulence often makes it difficult for you to see smaller flies, and the ability to see the fly is necessary to hook a high percentage of the fish that take. Some anglers drop down to a size 14 fly during the day, when visibility is good, and work back up to a size 10 at dusk. A bouyant, general-purpose fly, such as a Humpy (i.e. Goofus Bug, Horner Deer Hair), is usually a better choice in this type of water than one that imitates a particular insect.

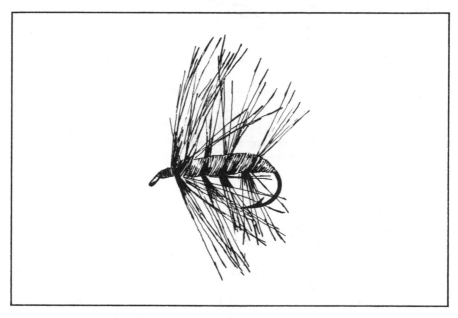

4-1: *Wrapping the hackle the length of a fly's body is called palmering. In this Orange Palmer the over-sized hackle contributes to the fly's enticing fluttery drift in mixed currents, which creates an impression of the wing-flapping behavior of egg-laying caddisflies and stoneflies.*

My favorite for this type of fishing is an old standard in northern California, a size 10 Orange Palmer. This fly is known elsewhere as the Orange Asher; it is a life-like imitation of egg-laying caddisflies and stoneflies. The long, stiff hackles wound the length of the hook shank not only help keep the fly up, but provide air resistance during the cast. This enables you to drop the fly gently, when using an unusually short leader. Other patterns, such as Bi-visibles, Variants and Spiders, share this feature and are effective in pocket water.

4-2: *Pocket-water dry fly anglers must often change position to keep fly, leader, and line on the same drift lane.*

The Approach

In short line methods where you must get close to the fish, the approach to the hole is very important. Trout, which face upcurrent to be able to see food drifting down toward them, are much more likely to see you when you wade down the stream than when you wade upstream from behind them.

But concealment from the trout includes more than approaching from behind. It also means keeping low, whether by submerging part of your body in wading, crouching low, dropping to one knee, or even crawling on your stomach. If a trout can see you as it turns upward toward the fly, or swims downstream in pursuit of the fly, you aren't low enough. Some anglers become so experienced at knowing how much a trout can see in a particular spot that they will save energy by hunching over only after their cast and only as much as necessary.

Casting position is determined not only by the need for concealment, but also by the need to achieve a "natural" drift of the fly—as if there were no leader attached to it. As a dry fly angler, the more you cast across the stream, the more the line and leader fall on currents that move at different speeds. If part of the line or leader gets ahead of the fly, it will pull the fly across stream, producing "drag." In order to prevent drag in mixed currents, you should attempt to get the fly, leader, and line to fall in the same drift lane so they all move at roughly

4-3: *Casting upstream and keeping low gets you close enough to present the fly where mixed currents prevent long drifts.*

the same speed. This means finding a casting position that permits you a cast aimed straight upstream or nearly so. The turbulence of surface currents in pocket water is often sufficient to conceal your leader from trout beneath it.

So the approach used here is quite different from that described for fishing the downstream angles of a wide riffle (Chapter 2). Here you buck the current, position yourself more precisely, and cast to "targets" unlike the systematic covering of one large run.

Casting Techniques

The angler who fishes short pools seems to be flicking line back and forth constantly, without any noticeable pause between back cast and forecast. This fast-casting rhythm is due primarily to two things: first, it takes almost no time to straighten 10 to 15 feet of line behind the rod; and second, some of the pools are so short that long drifts are impossible and so turbulent that repeated drifts are necessary to make sure the trout have seen the fly.

Pin-point accuracy in casting is often important in this fishing. George Dozier had an interesting way of teaching his 11 year old pupil this lesson. He would often invite me to make the first casts into particularly promising pools. When I would fail to raise a fish, he would shake his head as if he couldn't understand why a fish hadn't risen and then cast an identical pattern into what I thought was the same spot. Only this time a trout would rise to take the fly. The first few times this happened, I attributed it to my bad luck. But when it kept happening, I found myself beginning to notice differences in exactly where our flies were landing. Only then did I take fish. As nearly as possible you want to place your fly in a drift lane that moves it between about 6 and 12 inches a second.

There are at least two adjustments you can make to your basic cast for effective short-line dry fly fishing. One is to tilt the casting plane forward. The longer your fly rod, the more pronounced the forward tilt must be to drop the fly as close as 20 feet away. Lowering the plane of your forward cast to reach such nearby targets means that you must elevate your backcast, if you are to maintain the 180 degree separation between a straightened line behind you and a straightened line in front.

A second basic adjustment may be necessary when you have to present the fly under overhanging branches. Here you learn to cant or tilt the fly rod down to one side (the right side for a right handed caster) to make a sidearm cast. In doing this, your casting forearm is also canted to coincide with the angle of the fly rod. If necessary, you can also lower your right hip as a means of lowering the angle of the fly rod even farther. The line should unroll on the cast to form loops in a horizontal plane.

Eventually you become proficient in using the fly rod in various casting angles—sidearm, three-quarters overhead, almost vertical, and even tipped to the left side.

The presence of streamside foliage also teaches you to look back before casting. A slight change in the angle of the backcast may keep the fly from hanging up in a tree. At times the foliage is so thick that a backcast is impossible, and the roll cast (discussed in the previous chapter) or some shortline flip of the rod becomes necessary to present the fly.

Line-Handling and Fishing Techniques

Frequently line handling begins with the cast itself. When fishing short pools, your fly should land at about the same time the leader and line do. If the fly lands first, it may sink because nothing else has first absorbed the shock of landing on the water. If, however, your line and leader land much before the fly, they are drifting toward the fast water at the tail of the pool while the fly is still airborn—with the result that some of the fishable drift is lost. And the drifts are short enough already in pocket water.

One of the most difficult things about fishing a dry fly in short pools is that your concentration must be divided. On the one hand, you need to watch the fly itself for the earliest indication of a rising trout. But on the other hand you must watch the line at the point where it leaves the water. If part of the line is allowed to drift into the faster water at the

4-4: *Splitting concentration here refers to the need to watch the line to keep it lifted off fast water as well as the need to watch the drifting fly.*

tail of the pool where it tumbles into the next one, the line immediately picks up speed, pulls on the fly, and ruins the natural drift.

So it is important in this method—and in any upstream fly fishing method— to gather in line at the same speed the current brings it down to you. It is this element more than any other that makes upstream fly fishing more difficult intially than the two methods already described. The ability to strip in line fast enough to prevent the build-up of slack takes practice but is essential to setting the hook before the trout has had time to spit it out.

Though some anglers gather in line by means of the technique called the "hand twist" retrieve, I recommend stripping in line because it is easier for beginners to learn and more versatile.

One of the basic fishing concepts that has been handed down from one generation of flyrodders to the next asserts that the first cast to a pool is the one most likely to catch fish and that your chances diminish with each successive cast. This concept generally holds true in small streams or pocket water when fish are hungry. When trout are inactive, however, it sometimes pays off to work a good spot thorough - ly, as repeated casts seem to induce strikes from some trout.

Whenever trout begin to feed actively, the experienced angler is quick to sense the change in the stream's biology, and adjusts to it by moving upstream faster and making fewer casts to each pool. The underlying principle becomes one of fishing over as many hungry fish as possible during the "hot" period. In larger streams, where many fish occupy the same run, it may be better to move to the best holding water in that stretch and remain there.

There is a tendency for some beginners to want to remove the fly from the water if it has been poorly cast. This is usually a mistake, because even large fish can be taken on sloppy casts. Trout are not casting critics. However, there is a time when I will lift my fly off early in the drift—when it starts to sink from my view. In this kind of fishing, you strive to keep the fly visible in rough water. If it begins to sink, the fly is absorbing water which will spoil its flotation in subsequent drifts. Also a submerged fly is not visible in some light conditions, causing strikes to be missed that wouldn't be if the fly were visible.

The visibility of the fly is so important that pocket water anglers are forever doing things to dry it off, including false casting, reapplying flotants, absorbing the moisture in chamois-like cloths or commercial powders, changing flies, and even intentionally casting to hit a rock, so the fly will bounce off and land gently on the water. Snagging your fly in a tree will dry it off too—if you can get the fly back.

Hooking and Landing the Fish

If you fail to hook rising trout it can be for several reasons. A trout that suddenly turns and bolts away has probably seen you, indicating inadequate concealment. If the trout spits out the fly before the hook is set, either you weren't watching the fly or permitted excessive slack to form in the line on the water. Any time you set the hook at what seems to be the right moment, and the fish isn't hooked, you should develop the habit of checking to make sure the point isn't broken. The failure to do this may cost you other fish that day.

I learned this lesson the hard way. It was mid-June and a foot of snow covered the banks of little Foster Creek, 8000 feet high in the Sierra. I could tell from where the foot prints were positioned in the snow that the angler ahead of me was experienced and left handed (as I am). That angler left me little—only three fish rose to my fly that afternoon. It surprised me when I missed the first two, because the takes had been deliberate. I knew my timing was perfect on the third miss, but only then did I check and find the broken hook. It's interesting how well we learn when forced to walk home skunked.

If the small trout you hook come flying back toward you in the air, you have set with too much force. Such force will often break the tippet when larger fish are hooked. The hook should be set as gently as possible, and fish "played" back toward you under water by stripping in line. It is not necessary to reel in the slack line and "play the fish off the reel" unless you have hooked a large trout.

Wading and Safety

Many anglers learn their basic wading skills and thus develop confidence while fishing small streams, where the current force is not excessive and slips, seldom hazardous. To some people, the wading of a mountain stream is one of the most enjoyable features of the sport. The wading becomes essential to reach some of the best fish, whether in brush-lined brooks or midstream pockets of wide rivers.

Even in small, gentle streams, anglers soon learn to glue either felt or Ozite indoor-outdoor carpeting to the soles of their wading footgear to minimize slipping on smooth or algae-covered rocks.

Don't let yourself be tempted to hop from one dry rock to another on shallow streams. This is a dangerous practice because dry rocks can be slippery, and you could hit your head and drown in shallow water. Even dry, apparently safe footing should be tested before weight is fully transferred—particularly in the vicinity of a stream

This is also true of logs, which can be quite slippery. Log jams often provide the shortest route between point A and point B on those obstacle courses known as trout streams. However, insecure footing or rotting wood can cause you to fall through such jams and risk serious injury.

Variations of this Method

Many small streams have sections that are overgrown with alders or other moisture-loving, low-growing trees. Quite often these sections contain more and bigger trout than do accessible stretches and offer the opportunity of action well into the season as well as an escape from anglers who intrude on your solitude.

To catch fish in such places requires fighting through brush, crawling on hands and knees, and resorting to a no-cast, shortline version of dapping, where a foot or so of a very short leader may be all that drops from a rod tip poked between alder branches. It is not flyfishing as popularly conceived, but it can be great fun and quite instructive to a child learning the sport.

Once the basics of this short-line, dry fly method are learned, it should not be difficult for you to make a transition to longer casts and longer pools in your dry fly fishing. This subject is covered in Chapter 8.

4-5: *Tiny areas of quiet water between and around rocks are reached only by "dapping the fly." Pulsating hackles of flies dapped on the surface sometimes bring fish up from cover when nothing else will.*

Selected References

Betters, F. "Picking Pockets," *Fly Fisherman,* 1981, Mid-Season.

Flick, A. "How to Fish Pocket Water," in J. Migel (Ed.) *The Masters of the Dry Fly,* Philadelphia: Lippincott, 1977.

McClane, A.J. "All-Hackle—The Valuable Tackle," *Field & Stream,* 1974, September.

McClane, A.J., "The Dry Fly on Fast Water," *Field & Stream,* 1974, January.

5
A CAST-UPSTREAM
FISH-DOWNSTREAM
METHOD
FOR BIG NYMPHS
Coping with Big Water

The Fishing Situation

The combined current speed and depth of some trout water, whether in the form of choppy riffles or fast, smooth-topped glides, is sufficient to create a problem in getting your fly down to the bottom in time to attract fish. So distinctive adaptations must be made to the basic down-and-across sunken-fly method (described in Chapter 2) if you are to fish effectively in such big water.

5-1: *"Bottom Pockets" or depressions may be formed by ledges or large, submerged rocks.*

Trout in fast, deep runs are often large and generally hold where a big rock or a depression on the stream's bottom has created a niche of slow water. These "bottom pockets" are seldom visible from above the water's surface, and the fast surrounding currents tend to keep the fish close to home in their feeding. So we have "pockets" we can't see containing fish that don't move. The implication is to use a systematic method that provides a thorough coverage of the stream's bottom.

I remember a particular bottom pocket that "Polly" Rosborough alerted me to on the Williamson River in Oregon. As he described a pool he wanted me to try, he cautioned me that the biggest fish would be holding below an obvious boil on the water's surface. He said the boil and the depression the fish would be holding in were both formed by a large submerged rock. For some reason I didn't get to that pool until the next summer. My friend Dick Holland reached the water first, looked it over, and moved up to the head of the pool. When I arrived, I agreed that Dick had selected the best looking water, but I moved toward the tail of the pool to find Polly's boil. It turned out that Dick's water produced a feisty 14-inch rainbow, just seven inches shorter than the one I found. So my appreciation for bottom pockets and for a man known affectionately as "Polly" grew that day. And don't feel sorry for Dick; he took a four-and-a-half pound rainbow earlier that morning.

Rigging Adaptations

Our basic fly rod will catch fish with this method, but if you fish such water regularly, you will use a rod that does a better job of casting heavy flies. This latter rod typically takes a number 7 or 8 fly line, is 8½ to 9-feet long, and has a stiffer action throughout the butt section than our general-purpose rod.

The floating fly line will often be replaced by one designed to sink. The faster and deeper the water, the greater is the need for a sinking line. A hi-density sinking line will be most useful, though serious anglers often have several different types to be able to vary the sink rate when fishing different runs. Where casting distance is required to cover the far reaches of a heavy riffle, shooting-taper fly lines may be preferred. These short 30-foot fly lines can be purchased as is or fashioned by cutting the length off one end of a full-length, double-tapered fly line.

Leaders used with these sinking lines are typically short, between four and six feet in length. With so little distance between the fly and fly line, the sinking qualities of each combine to overcome any buoyancy in the leader. Longer leaders will keep the fly from sinking to bottom levels as quickly as you would like.

Leader tippet diameters may be .010 inch (1X) or larger as required to turn over a heavily-weighted fly in the cast as well as to hold big fish that use their weight and the force of the current against you when hooked.

The flies selected for such fast, heavy water are almost always big (e.g., sizes 2-8) and heavily weighted (e.g., hook shank wrapped with 2-5 amp lead fuse wire). A fly should be big enough to attract trout's attention in turbulent flow as well as to represent the mouthful of food it needs to replace the energy expended to catch the prey in fast current. It is also easier to add weight to the long shank of a big fly than to a smaller one of the same design. Coincidentally, the bottoms of these fast runs harbor large insects, crustaceans, and forage fish so the large flies are also fairly imitative.

Another feature of the fly that is considered important is that it appear to be alive. One way to achieve this impression of life in a fly that is drifting downstream, (rather than being jerked or moved across the current), is to use materials that will pulsate in the currents. Hackles tied along the shank of big flies do a good job of this and conceal the fact that the fly looks like nothing that ever lived.

I would guess that the big fly most commonly used in deep, fast runs is a weighted Wooly-Worm, with a black or brown body, tied on a size 4 or 6 hook. While the Wooly-Worm is a generalist pattern, knowledgeable anglers tend to select fly patterns that more closely resemble the most abundant, large foods in such water—big stoneflies or sculpins.

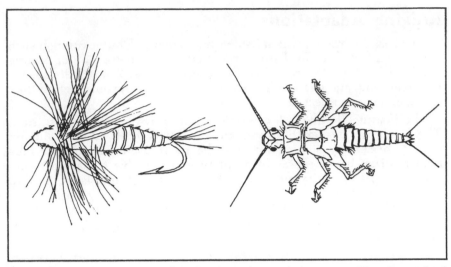

5-2: *Large meals are associated with trout in big, turbulent water. Heavily-weighted flies, such as the Brook's Montana Stone, resemble fast-water stonefly nymphs in size, shape, and color.*

The Approach

Stealth is less important in this kind of fly fishing than in any other. The turbulence of heavy, fast water and the bottom-holding tendencies of the fish permit you to make an approach from up and across stream. This is fortunate because an upstream-cast fly in fast water moves downstream past you so quickly that downstream fishing angles are required to achieve a sufficiently long drift to attract fish.

As in the basic down-and-across swing, the typical progression is to fish from the head of the pool to the tail, stopping every few steps to cover the water from near to far. A long run of a good-sized river will take an hour or more to fish with such thorough coverage.

Casting Requirements

Although the fishing occurs downstream of you, casts are quartered up and across the stream in this method. The combined depth and current speed require an upstream cast, the purpose of which is to provide time for the fly to reach the bottom while still upstream of the trout. Although the cast is angled upstream, your feet should be planted to face down and across stream—the direction you will be facing when the fly reaches the fish.

The cast should be made with a large, open loop from a rod angled well off to the side of vertical. Both the loop and the rod angle should help to keep the heavily-weighted fly away from your head. My teaching requirement that students wear a hat and sunglasses to

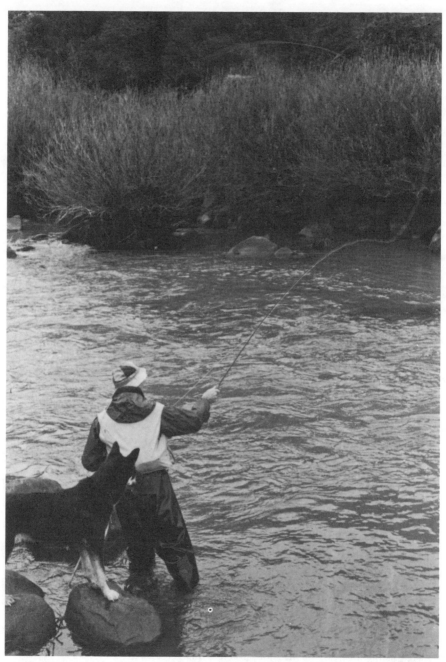

5-3: *A large, open loop is cast when you need to keep a weighted leader away from your head.*

protect the head and eyes becomes particularly important when casting heavy flies.

A casting variation sometimes referred to as a "tension cast" becomes useful in covering the far side of wide riffles. The tension is created by allowing the weighted terminal tackle (i.e., weight on leader and/or fly) to trail just under the surface once the line has straightened downstream at the completion of the drift. Then, when power is applied smoothly in the forward cast, this tension bends the rod. As the line comes off the water and the cast is completed, the fly is propelled a considerable distance up and across stream. The best description of this cast I know of can be found n Charles Brooks' book, *Nymph Fishing for Larger Trout* (p. 128).

Line-Handling and Fishing Techniques

After the upstream cast, the fly sinks and drifts through water that was already fished from farther upstream. So don't expect strikes until the fly has drifted opposite you or some distance downstream of your position. But you should already be doing some line-handling as the fly is drifting down toward you. If you fail to do so, slack will form in the line underwater with the result that too many strikes will go undetected. Some inexperienced flyrodders attempt to minimize this problem by stripping the line as it approaches them from above, and then

5-4: *Casting upstream (to the right) provides time for a fly to sink before being fished in the heavy riffle off to the angler's left. The dark rock under the caster's arm serves as a reference point for this series of three photos.*

are faced with another problem of feeding line out again as the fly moves away downstream. Otherwise they don't have enough line out to reach the trout below.

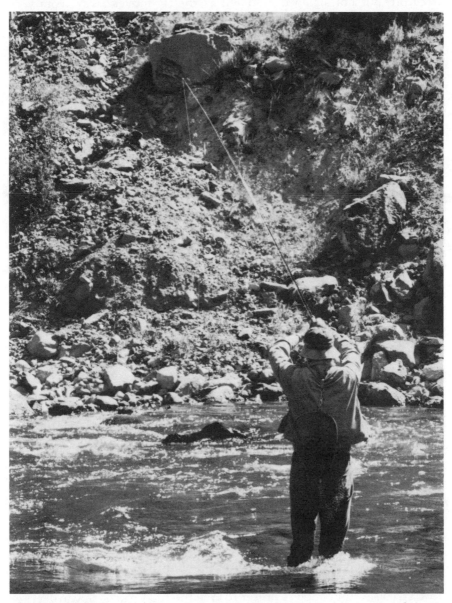

5-5: *Raising the fly rod and arms "a la Brooks," keeps extra line off the water when the fly is closest to you.*

A better way to solve this problem is to lift the line off the water as it comes toward you from upstream by raising the fly rod and arms as much as necessary. The line that would be forming slack underwater is lifted off, but not stripped in. Then as the fly moves away from you downstream, this line becomes available again as you lower the rod and arms and lay the line back on the water as straight as possible. All this while, the fly has had time to sink to the bottom. In my opinion, the development and popularization of this rod-handling technique is Charles Brooks' most important contribution to fly fishing.

Strikes may come during the ensuing drift or when the fly swings across stream below you. The retrieve or next cast should be delayed for several seconds until the fly has had time to catch up with the line.

5-6: *When the fly is downstream and the line is lowered again, you are ready to begin fishing.*

So in this method, you first try to get the fly deep, then allow it to tumble freely or "dead drift" for a distance, until the line tightens and swings the fly across the current toward you. The fly may be activated as you retrieve for the next cast. However, most anglers also impart some sort of action to the fly throughout the drift, at least at times. Some give an occasional strip with the line hand during the drift because they believe it enables them to maintain a tight line and detect more strikes. Other anglers prefer to give the rod tip little upward jerks without retrieving, a method that allows them to continue to use all the line that was cast throughout the drift and still impart action to the fly.

Still others pull with the line hand and move the rod simultaneously to reduce the amount of subsurface slack or bend in the swinging line as they impart action.

Hooking and Landing Techniques

If you frequent heavy waters and use bit-fly methods, you soon learn to keep your hooks sharpened for the quickest penetration of hook points. The strong tippets permit you to strike vigorously, often double strike to assure that a big hook is firmly set. Large trout hooked downstream of you often move farther in that direction and gain a considerable headstart. Frequently it becomes necessary to wade ashore and get downstream of the fish so that when it moves away from you it must fight the current as well as your fly rod.

The decision of whether to play the fish from midstream or wade ashore is not always easy to make. It involves a quick analysis of the amount of line the fish has taken out, the type of water the fish is moving through, and the toughness of the wade.

5-7: *Submerge the net before bringing the fish toward you. Avoid sudden swiping or reaching motions that could further alarm a half-exhausted trout.*

Should you decide to net the fish in midstream, it is important to develop the habit of lifting with the net, rather than reaching or swiping with it. The net is placed underwater, the fish is maneuvered over it, and then the net is lifted.

5-8: *Soon to be released, this trout should not be dropped into the deep part of the net. Injury could result from its entanglement in the mesh.*

Choose a net that will handle the largest fish you are likely to catch. Many rivers hold trout in excess of 20 inches, so the frame of the net should be sturdy and the net bag at least 22 inches deep.

Wading and Safety

The water fished by this method can be among the most dangerous of trout waters to the wading angler. The same depth and fast currents that have led to adjustments in basic fishing techniques also lead to adjustments in wading. Felt soles and a wading staff may no longer offer sufficient protection. Metal grids, studs, chains, or sandals are widely used for added protection against slipping, and a flotation vest may save your life when slipping does occur.

Advanced Variations

No one has done more to systematize heavy-water nymph fishing than Charles Brooks. One of the most enjoyable days I have spent on trout water was with this knowledgeable, friendly man. I only regret that I didn't have the forethought to film his demonstration of the "Brooks Method." Variations of this method are discussed in some detail in his books.

This method for fishing big nymphs also works with streamers—patterns tied to imitate small fish. In imitating the movements of small

5-9: *A grid-footed angler has extra protection against slippage in fast water. The Muncie Grid (on his right foot) and Korker both work well in most situations.*

fish, the fly is typically acitivated rather than "dead drifted" as is commonly done when imitating nymphs.

The most successful streamer fisherman I know, Dick Holland, prefers to fish them with a floating line. His technique includes a long up-and-across stream cast, a huge mend to throw the line upstream, and some short upstream spurts of the fly interspersed with additional mends during the fly's downstream drift. He gets a high percentage of takes prior to the swing of the fly across stream, whereas less-experienced anglers usually rely on the swing itself for their action.

Selected References

Brooks, C.E. *Nymph Fishing for Larger Trout.* New York: Crown, 1976.
Brooks, C.E. *The Trout and the Stream.* New York: Crown, 1974.
Wixom, H. "How to Fish Swift Water," *Cord Sport Facts-Fishing Report,* 1975.

꧁꧁꧁꧁꧁꧁꧁꧁꧁꧁꧁꧁꧁꧁꧁꧁꧁꧁꧁

6
LAKE FISHING WITH A
SINKING FLY LINE
Going Down After Them

꧁꧁꧁꧁꧁꧁꧁꧁꧁꧁꧁꧁꧁꧁꧁꧁꧁꧁꧁

The Fishing Situation

Lake-dwelling trout do not always feed at the surface. Frequently they may feed so deep that the fly fishing methods described in Chapter 3 no longer work. Under such conditions, many "generalists" among the angling fraternity soon put their spin-fly rods to the use for which they seem designed—spin fishing. However, the person who is deeply committed to fly fishing, who loves the feel of a fly rod, simply changes from a floating fly line to a sinking fly line.

When trout are not rising in lakes, you face the problem of finding them. Surface rises enable you to *know* the water you fish contains trout. But when fish are no longer visible, you begin to *hope* the water you cast to contains trout. This situation is typical of mountain lakes when the bright light of midday induces the trout to seek the protection of deep water. These trout may continue to feed, but now look for subsurface food.

Even when fish are feeding near the surface, a strong wind moves your floating fly line and fly unnaturally, with the result that trout begin to ignore the fly. A slow-sinking or intermediate fly line will cut down through the water enough to avoid being pushed around by the wind and yet permit you to fish a fly near the surface. This is only one of the conditions that requires you to have a sinking line when fly fishing in lakes.

I remember with chagrin my first exposure to little Martis Lake near Truckee, California shortly after it opened to no-kill fly fishing. Frank Collin was anxious to have me fish an effective technique he had put together there, but somehow forgot to mention it involved the use of a sinking line. It turned out that Frank had a spare, but we still ended up one sinking line short in our party. As a charitable gesture I agreed to start out with a floating line. By the time someone offered to let me use a sinking line, the action was 90% over. If I had that day to live over, I doubt very much that I would have started with a floating line.

Rigging Adaptations

Our general-purpose fly rod performs adequately in this type of fly fishing. Many lake specialists are backpacking anglers who prefer that the cases for their fly rods not extend beyond the height of their backpacks. Therefore backpacking fly rods typically break down into three, four, or five pieces, and are much more enjoyable rods to cast than spin-fly combination rods.

The type of sinking line selected may depend on the characteristics of a particular lake you fish on a regular basis; some lakes slope more gradually near shore than others, for example. If you fish a number of different lakes on the same trip, you gain flexibility by carrying at least slow-sinking and fast-sinking lines in addition to the basic floating line. To conserve space, some backpackers use only 30-foot shooting-taper lines and carry the extra lines coiled up. Held in these coils by short pieces of pipe cleaner and having a pre-tied loop in the heavy end, these short lines can be changed quickly while fishing. You will probably find that a number 7 shooting-taper balances best with a number 6 fly rod, because there is almost no line weight to be cast beyond the first 30-feet of fly line. Full-length fly lines continue to have more weight beyond this point.

There is nothing sacred about 30 feet of line. In fact many accomplished double-haul casters prefer 35 to 45-foot lengths. These casters have the ability to control the extra line beyond the rod tip and are able to pick up additional casting distance with it. The added length in a 45 foot line also makes it possible to roll cast farther. On the other hand, some backpackers prefer ultra-short 25-foot shooting-tapers because of limited backcasting room.

There is considerable variation in leader lengths used by sinking line anglers. The absense of fast stream currents eliminates the need for very short leaders. Often standard 7½ to 9-foot leaders are used, though I see many successful lake specialists using 12-foot leaders with 5X or 6X tippets and small nymphs in the size 14 to 18 range.

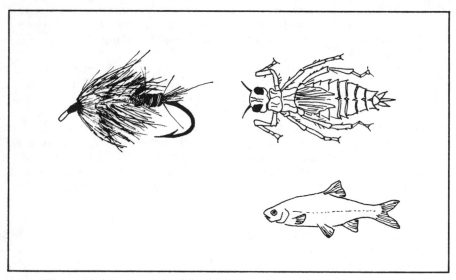

6-1: *The perfect big nymph for lake fishing would pass for leech, dragonfly nymph, and minnow. The closest we come is in general patterns such as Polly Rosborough's Casual Dress or modified Wolly-Worms, such as the Wooly-Bugger.*

Some of the same "searching" patterns that we discussed in relation to stream fishing are effective in lakes. The subtle-toned Hare's Ear Nymph resembles a variety of the common, small-sized life forms found in lakes, including mayfly nymphs, caddisfly larva and pupa, scud, and water boatmen. Large, dark Wooly-Worms tied with soft hackle, or large, shaggy, impressionistic nymphs sometimes cover a range of the larger trout food in lakes, including dragon fly nymphs, bait fish, and leeches. You can also find fly patterns that imitate each of these items specifically.

6-2: *Sketching lake features from a high overlook records the "big picture" that is not visible when fishng.*

The Approach

The trail into a remote lake may afford an overview of the water to be fished. You may find it worthwhile to stop at such places to draw a sketch of the main features of the lake for later reference when fishing. Inlets and outlets, points and coves, deep drop-offs, stream channels, submerged ridge lines, and weedbeds are among the features that contribute to successful fishing. Of course any information you can obtain about the lake, its trout, or food chain, prior to the trip by writing the managing agency is all to the good.

When trying to locate trout with a sinking line, you will want to find a spot with deep water close to shore; sometimes a steep bank provides this, but interferes with a back cast. A protruding point of land may also be a good place to start, and not primarily because backcasts are easier to make there. The reason lies in the fact that you may be able to fish over two different groups of cruising fish from the same spot. Some experienced lake anglers have found that trout cruising a shoreline will turn around and go back the other way upon reaching the submerged point or ridge, rather than to continue straight ahead into deeper water or to make the sharp turn necessary to continue around the ridge. Trout cruising to the same ridge from the opposite direction are also likely to turn around and go back the way they came, providing you with the second group of fish.

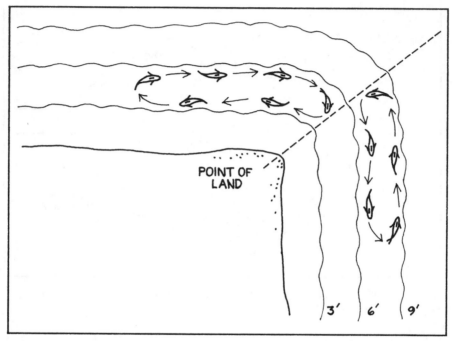

6-3: *A point of land may place you within reach of two groups of cruising fish.*

A strong wind may chase you to a protected cove, though there are several different theories about how to fly fish in the wind. When possible, I prefer to move to a shoreline that permits me to cast into the wind. Though casting range is reduced by doing this, any insects on the water will be blown toward you and will become concentrated close to your shore. Also the wave action sometimes stirs up additional food from the shallow bottom there. Trout learn to find concentrations of food and, if not foraging actively, will face into the current from where their food and your artificial fly are coming. So the wind can be made to work for you.

Marv Taylor, one of the better known lake flyrodders in the Rocky Mountain area follows similar thinking in working submerged shorelines during windy conditions. He believes that trout will move to the protected side of submerged ridges, face the current, and let the wind bring food to them.

Casting Techniques

One thing you can do when faced with the problem of locating trout in a lake is to sample various depths. Another approach, if you are limited to wading or bank fishing, is to cover as much distance as possible. This means casting a long line and fishing long drifts. The goal of extending your fishable range may lead you to learn the double haul, a technique that increases casting distance, some say by up to 30 percent over what can be obtained with the rod hand alone.

In the double haul, the line hand contributes to distance and line speed by pulling or hauling line twice during the cast—once as the rod hand applies power to the backcast and again as it applies power to the forecast. After the second pull, the line hand releases its grip so that the line at the angler's feet is free to move up through the guides of the rod to follow that which is already moving toward the middle of the lake.

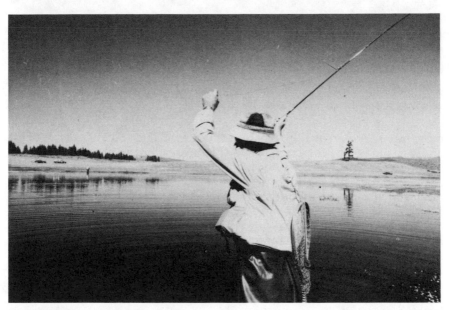

6-4: *Double-hauling adds distance to your casts. With backcast and first haul completed, the line hand has drifted up toward the rod in preparation for the second haul.*

When using a sinking line, you combine the double haul with a roll cast. The double haul provides the distance and the roll cast efficiently returns the sunken line to the surface for the next double haul. Thus, the whole sinking line doesn't have to be stripped in, but can be recast when 30 feet of line is still beyond the rod tip.

The double haul requires enough coordination between both arms that personal assistance should be sought when first learning the

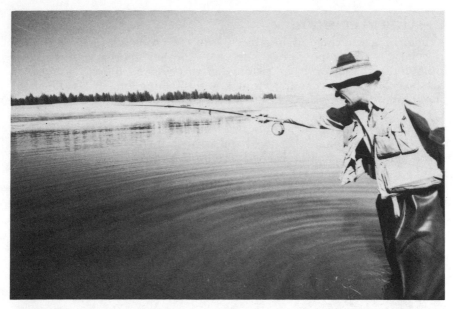

6-5: *During the forward cast the line has been hauled down and back. When the line is released, it will shoot out through the rod guides.*

movements. If personal instruction is not available at a local tackle shop or fly fishing club, you might benefit from reading an article written by Mel Krieger. Mel has developed a part method, or "pantomine" method that simplifies the learning of this cast. This method, and the movements involved are laid out systematically in the Winter 1980 issue of *Flyfisher.*

Casting into the wind, as suggested earlier in this chapter, requires some modification in technique. The double haul is useful in this situation because it increases line speed, which contributes to your ability to cut through wind. Without the ability to double haul, you can still fight the wind by using a casting variation sometimes referred to as "casting with the butt of the fly rod." In this "butt cast" your casting hand drives downward and forward more than usual to get as much flex out of the rod's butt section as possible. This difference becomes apparent when contrasted to the movement of casting a dry fly with 25 feet of line and only the tip half of the fly rod bending appreciably. This is sometimes referred to as "casting off the tip of the rod." Both the butt cast and a tip cast can be useful in fly fishing and should be practiced.

Line-Handling and Fishing Techniques

The basic technique for locating the depth at which trout are feeding is to count while the line is sinking. The count ends when you begin the retrieve. Different depths are sampled systematically by varying this count till you begin to get strikes.

6-6: *A submerged rod tip assures the precise movement of a fly fished on a sinking line.*

Immediately after the cast, you should lower the tip of the rod. When sinking lines are used, you should consider submerging the rod up to half its length. I always thought this technique was unnecessary until fellow fly fishing teacher, Scott Henderson, and I conducted some experiments in a swimming pool. Only then did I realize the extent to which the submerged rod tip adds to your control over the exact movements of the fly. Like many anglers, I had assumed that stripping in 8 inches of line with the line hand would move the fly 8 inches at the same rate of movement. To my surprise, this happened only with the tip submerged. Even with the tip held a couple of inches above the surface and 40 feet of fly line out, an 8 inch strip of line resulted in moving the fly an average of only 4 inches. What happens is that slack forms in the submerged line, and the first 4 inches of the pull accomplish little more than tightening the line. Only the second 4 inches of the strip actually move the fly 4 inches. Then, between strips, the fly may drift a few more inches as the line accumulates slack once again.

It's even worse when the tip is held 2 feet above the surface. A series of 8-inch strips, with momentary pauses interspersed between, is transmitted as almost constant, steady movement of the fly rather than the expected stop-and-go jerks. You might just as well use a slow hand-twist retrieve. If you are interested in imitating the specific movements of small, invertebrate life, it would be worth your time to observe your fly moving through the depths of a swimming pool.

Some fly patterns seem to be most effective with particular retrieves. For example, a Matuka type of streamer looks very enticing when moved erratically in still water—it looks good even between jerks when completely still in the water. On the other hand, a streamer with marabou tied in only at the head of the fly looks ridiculous sitting dead in quiet water, with the marabou separated from the fly's body. It looks much more appealing (to the human eye at least) when permitted to move continuously. The currents of streams undoubtedly contribute to the effectiveness of this pattern.

Hooking and Landing Techniques

Fishing with a submerged rod tip minimizes the amount of slack in the line and thus contributes to quickness in setting the hook. Some lake anglers avoid striking upward with the rod because they feel most of the power is absorbed in lifting an inert line from the surface. They believe that rod power is transmitted more efficiently to the fly by moving the line laterally against water drag. So they set the hook with a short rod movement to one side.

When using a sinking line in lakes, you may find yourself hooking larger fish than you are accustomed to. Sometimes large fish in lakes move slowly when hooked and panic only when first led into shallow water. Under these conditions it is wise to expect not to beach the fish the first time it is worked into shallow water. Expect it to bolt into deep water with renewed energy, and you won't make the mistake of trying to overpower it at this critical moment—when a tippet can easily be broken.

Wading and Safety

When wading in lakes you should always be alert for sudden drop-offs, or unevenness in soft-bottomed areas. These drop-offs may be concealed under weedbeds you are walking on or by water that has been discolored by your movements. You should move carefully when wading in unfamiliar surroundings.

Variations of this method

You can build on this sinking line method by experimenting with different lines and retrieves until you find the best combination for your particular lake. Even this may vary as the season progresses. If you take to this form of fishing, you will feel the need to cover more water and will obtain a float tube, small boat or both. As an added bonus, you will find that many good trout lakes are usually closer to metropolitan areas than are good trout streams.

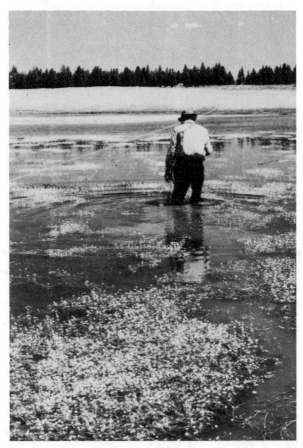

6-7: *Trudging through the weedbeds should be done carefully as they may conceal drop offs.*

Selected References

Bates, J. *Streamers & Bucktails—The Big Fish Flies.* New York: Knopf, 1979.

Blanton, D. "Sinking Lines," *Fly Fisherman,* 1979, Early Season.

Blanton, D. "Sinking Lines for Stillwater Trout," *Fly Fisherman,* 1979, Mid-Season.

Harrop, R. "The Feather-Belly Matuka," *Rod and Reel,* 1981, January/ February.

Havstad, J. "Sink Rate of Sinking Lines," *The Flyfisher,* 1979, Fall.

Janssen, H. "The Life of a Damsel," *Angler,* 1980, Late Spring.

Krieger, M. "Down Up and the Double Haul," *Flyfisher,* 1980, Winter.

McClane, A.J. "Match-the-Minnow," *Field and Stream,* 1968, July.

Moyle, P. and Baltz, D. "Stillwaters West," In J. Merwin (Ed.), *Stillwater Trout.* Garden City, New York: Doubleday, 1980.

7

SHORT LINE, WET FLY FISHING

A Transition To Upstream Nymphing

The Fishing Situation

For many people the most enjoyable way to fish "pocket water" is with a dry fly, as described in Chapter 4. However, I believe that the most productive way to fish this water is with a sunken fly—either a wet fly or nymph. There are two many times throughout the day and too many days throughout the season that fish are reluctant to rise but can be taken with a fly fished near the bottom. And it took me many years to prove to myself that the better fish in this type of cascading water, the ones I most want to hook, are primarily bottom feeders—especially in the deeper, protected holds.

For years I fished dry flies only and gave little thought to wet fly anglers, until I saw some highly skilled short-line nymphers at work. I soon realized that the added dimension of depth brought with it some intriguing challenges as well as the increased action. The challenge of presenting the fly with the optimal combination of depth, naturalness, and line control is more involved than you would think from the short lengths of line typically used.

The short length and narrowness of the small pools as well as the extreme current variations in these restricted areas present some problems. How do you get the fly deep quickly and yet keep it moving naturally in the water? How do you detect strikes in pocket water without the advantage of seeing them on the surface? These problems require some adjustments in fishing technique as well as in tackle.

Rigging Adaptations

Some of the modifications in tackle that are suggested here are the same as those suggested for fishing pocket water with a dry fly. In both methods short casts are made to keep line from falling on the fast currents surrounding the small pools. It is this use of a short line that leads to modifications in fly rod and leader: the fly rod should be soft enough in action to "load" or flex in response to the weight of only a few feet of line. The leader must be kept short to provide as much line weight beyond the rod tip as possible to help power the short casts. Seven and a half foot leaders or less are standard with this method.

Although a fly is fished deep with this method, floating fly lines are the rule. Depth is achieved by applying weight to the leader and the fly, rather than with a sinking line, which is more appropriate in broad expanses of water or when the current is less swift.

I recommend to my beginning students that they buy a package or two of flat lead wire strips (i.e., twistons) and that they spiral-wrap four or five turns of this lead wire and crimp the ends 18 inches above the fly. Wine bottle lead seals could also be cut into strips for this purpose. The flies I use with this method also have a half-dozen turns of 2-amp lead fuse wire under the body. So a moderate amount of weight is distributed in two places. If this weight were concentrated in one place, casting would become unwieldy and the drift, less natural.

For anglers already experienced in other fly fishing methods, I suggest replacing the weight on the leader with a second weighted fly. With two flies you can experiment continually with two different patterns and two different depths.

Beginners may use the two fly rigging, but usually they either dislike losing two good flies at once or shy away from a rigging that increases their likelihood of getting tangled or wrapped around everything within casting distance.

A simple way of rigging two flies is to use a blood knot to connect the last two sections of leader tippet material—a 1X (.010 inch) to a 3X (.008 inch) tippet section, for example. In tying this blood knot, the 1X material is tied to leave 6 to 8 inches of material extending beyond the knot. When tightened, this piece is not trimmed off and becomes the dropper strand. If tied correctly, it should extend straight out from the leader. Its stiffness keeps it away from the leader enough to prevent some tangling. It is crucial that the dropper strand be made from the thicker of the two sections.

At the end of the dropper strand, I often tie on a light-colored fly to imitate the lighter color tones that are characteristic of a variety of emerging insects. This is logical since the dropper is closer to the surface than is the "point fly." A Leisenring Spider, tied with a body of rabbit fur and hackled with grouse or partridge, is one of my favorites. Often I contrast this with a dark pattern on the tail or point fly fished

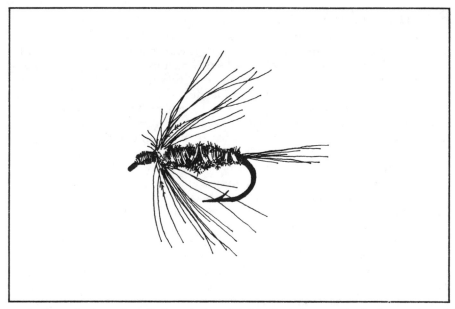

7-1: *Sparsely-dressed, well-chewed Gray-Hackle Peacock resembles both aquatic and terrestrial insects.*

near the bottom. My favorite fly for this purpose is a weighted Gray-Hackle Peacock—as good a pocket water fly as there is, in my estimation. The peacock herl makes a buggy-looking body that reflects light and appears translucent in sunlight. In rugged Western streams, a stiffer hackle is used for these flies than in the soft-hackled patterns preferred by many Eastern anglers.

The Approach

Most experienced pock-water anglers, whether they use surface or sunken flies, take advantage of the concealment afforded by approaching an upstream-facing trout from behind and casting up and across stream.

While I do this in my own fishing, I have found that fishing upstream angles with a sunken fly is too difficult for many beginners. There is just too much to learn at once about line-handling and strike detection. So I have developed a simplified approach to help make a smooth transition from downstream wet fly fishing to upstream wet fly fishing.

This "transition" method retains some of the familiar techniques of the basic down-and-across swing, while introducing some of the elements of upstream nymphing. This is accomplished by fishing across-stream angles, rather than upstream angles.

What I do is to find a pocket that can be approached from across stream and wade with the student to a point directly across-stream

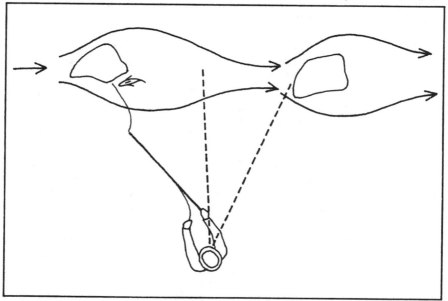

7-2: *"Bisecting the fishable drift" means positioning yourself with half the fishable water upstream of you and half downstream.*

from the pocket, so that exactly half of its fishable drift is upstream of the student, and half is downstream. I refer to this positioning concept as "bisecting the fishable drift."

7-3: *An across-stream "transition" to upstream nymphing affords the opportunity for both upstream and downstream fishing angles.*

The student casts up and across to the head of the pool and learns upstream techniques during the first half of the drift, and still has the familiar downstream fishing angles for the last half. There is a good chance that fish will continue to be hooked on the downstream side of the drift while students are putting together the more complicated upstream concepts. Eventually they begin to hook fish on the upstream side of the drift and gain the confidence needed to switch to drifts that are entirely upstream of them.

Students frequently ask me how close they should stand to the fishable water in a small pool. It's easy enough to answer, "as close as possible without spooking trout," but a learner has to spend time on the stream to fully understand what is involved. If you don't have a fishing friend to assist you in this, it may be worth your while to hire a fishing guide for a day. A competent guide can give you enough assistance and instruction in one day to help you overcome a number of shortcomings in your technique.

If no guide is available, you should keep a few things in mind about positioning yourself. First, there may be one best place to stand to cast to a particular piece of water. If your fly lands short of the mark in the fast water on your side of the pocket, you may need to take a step or two toward the fishable water. If you see fish dart around in the pocket, you have probably spooked them by being too close.

Each pocket is unique to a degree. Those with large areas of quiet water give the trout the best chance to see you. Any turbulent water on your side of the pocket can help conceal you from the trout. When in doubt, lower your silhouette.

A single step to one side or the other can be important in decreasing the amount of glare you see on the water. A second step can make it much easier to see your leader and detect strikes.

Exact positioning before the cast can add to the number of fish you catch or at least to the number of strikes you are able to detect.

Casting Techniques

Some flyrodders dislike fishing short line methods, especially when some weight is added to the terminal tackle. Yet if you enjoy wading mountain streams and catching large trout on a fly in mixed currents, the chances are you will add this method to your arsenal.

Many people practice casting on a lawn, usually with from 25 to 50 feet of fly line beyond the rod tip. Yet it is quite a different matter to prepare students for a pocket water experience. Pre-trip casting practice should include some time with weight on the leader and fly and only 10 to 20 feet of line beyond the rod tip. With an emphasis on

7-4: *Stopping the rod high on the tuck cast creates the high pivot point that allows the weighted fly to swing back toward you under the line.*

accuracy—a waste basket makes a convenient target—you begin to realize what is necessary to cast well in cascading water.

This emphasis on accuracy has to do with the extreme current variation that sometimes characterizes pocket water. A fly that lands six inches off target may drift much faster than you like, and the speed your fly moves through the water is directly related to the number of trout that move to your fly. It's amazing how trout will sometimes ignore one presentation after another until your fly finally lands in the narrow slot of slow water you have been aiming for; only then comes the hit. This is related to the fact that "naturalness" of drift in deep nymphing is a matter of matching the speed of bottom currents, which are typically much slower than those at the water's surface. Naturalness, under these conditions may be achieved by adding, rather than removing, terminal weight. As pointed out here, it is also achieved by accurate casting.

7-5: *Overpowering the cast helps to "tuck" the fly back toward you so it sinks quickly.*

A "specialty cast" that is useful in pocket water, when it is important to get the fly deep quickly, is commonly known as the tuck cast. The idea of this cast is to get the fly into the water first in such a way that the leader doesn't restrict the penetration of the fly down through the water. There are two important elements to the tuck cast. First, you overpower the forecast so that the leader not only straightens, but continues beyond straightening until the fly has swung under the line and "tucked" back toward you. Second, the forecast is stopped early so that the rod tip is high (i.e., 10 to 11 o'clock). A high rod tip enables the tuck to be completed above the surface of the water.

Line-Handling and Fishing Techniques

Sometimes it's more important to cast for "line control" than for depth. In fishing an upstream-cast sunken fly back toward you, you want to minimize the slack in the line or leader, both above and below the water's surface. This is because you must see rather than feel the indication of a strike. This is discussed in more depth in the next section. The implication is that the cast must be powered hard enough to straighten the leader on and into the water, so it is relatively straight as it sinks and trout take your fly.

7-6: *A low follow through on the cast provides line control rather than depth. The whole leader lands and starts to sink at the same time—with little slack.*

The weight on the terminal tackle, which provides depth to the drifting fly, also contributes to line control because its downward pull on the leader removes slack.

I see many beginners lose line control immediately by casting more line than is necessary to fish a particular spot. If extra line is cast, it forms hidden slack in the leader below the surface, which removes your ability to detect strikes. The two-fly concept discussed earlier reduces this possibility as long as you keep the top or dropper fly visible, near the surface. It is also a convenient check on the amount of leader that lies below.

You can check your tendency to cast too little line by watching to make sure the fly doesn't jerk upward through the water as you lift the rod tip after the cast.

Once the cast has been made, the line is controlled by the actions of your line hand and rod hand. As in other upstream fly fishing methods, the line hand works to keep slack from forming in the line that lays on the water upstream of you. This gathering in of line in pace with the current gains importance as your casts are angled more directly upstream.

7-7: *Raising the rod after the cast helps control above-surface slack as the fly approaches you.*

However, it is the work of the rod hand that is distinctive in this method. Immediately after the cast, the rod tip is smoothly lifted, which tends to straighten the line falling to the water's surface. The shorter the line being fished, the higher the rod tip is held and the more vertical the line and leader drop to and through the surface. In very close fishing; the leader cuts directly through the surface without any of it lying on the water. Sometimes the rod tip is raised during the drift, as the fly approaches you, and then lowered again to prolong the drift as it moves away. If you fail to raise the tip immediately after the cast when fishing this technique, you will lose many fish without even being aware that your fly had been taken.

As the rod tip is raised, it must be steadied as soon as possible. Then any unusual movement in your leader has been caused from below—by a trout or rock that has momentarily interrupted the movement of your fly. Whichever it is, you should set the hook immediately.

Though held steady, the rod tip is moved gradually to remain pointed toward your fly throughout the drift. This provides an element of naturalness to the drift as the fly is free to move directly downstream as if unattached to any leader. This "dead drift" dimension disappears

7-8: *Ted Fay's constant line control increases hooking percentages in pocket water. The line hand release on the cast enables him to pick line up again next to the rod, affording the longest possible distance for a single draw of the line. The fly can be activated during the drift by "feathering the line" as it is drawn to the side.*

quickly if the rod tip is allowed to precede the fly downstream or lag behind it.

A rod tip that lags behind the fly results in a tight line, which in turn brings the fly up to the surface when you want it drifting deep. A rod tip that leads the fly downstream may soon be pulling it faster than the speed of the current and therefore faster than the trout's food usually moves.

There are times, however, when it pays to pull the fly slightly faster than the current (or slightly across the current)—sacrificing some naturalness for increased line control. When fish are taking softly, for example, or when glare makes it difficult to see your leader, the increased line tension from pulling the fly provides the earliest possible feel of a take. There are days when this tight-line modification will result in fewer strikes, but a higher hooking percentage and more fish to catch and release.

This tight line adaptation is also useful when current variation is not extreme. By pulling slightly on the fly throughout the drift, so it moves gradually across stream toward you, the leader is kept fairly straight despite some current variation. This is an entirely different approach than extending your leader and fly over fast water. In the first case you are fishing through current variation; in the second, you are reaching over, and thus avoiding, the current variation.

Hooking and Landing the Fish

The transition from downstream sunken fly fishing to upstream sunken fly fishing is a transition from tactile strike detection to visual strike detection. A fly line that has tightened downstream of you permits strikes to be felt quickly whereas a line moving toward you from upstream tends to form slack, which gives the trout time to spit out the fly before the feel reaches your hands. Here you sense the strike sooner by seeing an unusual movement in the leader, before it even reaches the fly line.

Though excessive slack is to be avoided, there should be a slight bow in the line and leader dropping from the high rod tip. This bow or sag in the leader disappears whenever the movement of the fly is interrupted— whether by trout, snag, or sudden change in current speed. I like to watch my leader as close to the water as possible for the first indication of this straightening or tightening in the leader.

In upstream, sunken fly fishing, I set the hook by separating my hands—moving the rod to one side and pulling the line away to the other. Pulling with the line hand only won't set the hook if enough slack has formed in the line. And setting with the rod hand only makes it too easy to over-react and break fine tippets when big fish hit on a short line. The one time I set the hook with the rod hand only is when my whole rod arm is extended to reach a distant pocket.

7-9: *When nymphing upstream with a short line, watch your leader close to the water for the earliest indication of strikes.*

A big fish hooked in cascading water can be expected to move downstream through the entire series of rapids. In this situation you try to wade ashore and scramble down the bank with rod held high to keep as much line off the water as possible. When the line catches on a rock, it becomes a race to free the line before the fish can free itself. You look downstream for a pool large enough to catch up with the fish and beach or net it.

Wading and Safety

The most common wading problem I have when moving upstream through cascading water is tripping on submerged rocks. Falling upstream in shallow water is not usually dangerous, but can lead to scraped shins. This happens to me through ovrconfidence and by "striding"—alternating one foot in front of the other. What I should do is take the time to shuffle crablike, keeping the same foot upstream in my movements as I do when the water is fast and deep.

Wading staffs and felt-soled footgear are standard equipment for pocket-water anglers, and metal sandals or studs will give additional protection against slippery bottoms. The wading staff is particularly useful in locating odd-shaped or protruding rocks beneath frothy or discolored water and in dislodging flies snagged on obstruction.

7-10: *Over-sized pants on top of light-weight stocking-foot waders protect them from tearing.*

Variations of this Method

One particularly effective form of this method involving the use of two flies and short leaders has been popularized over the years by Ted Fay on the Upper Sacramento and McCloud Rivers in California. Fishing the two-fly rig has enabled Ted to experiment continually with fly patterns and learn which flies work best there throughout the season. For decades Ted Fay has given of his knowledge willingly. His assistance and friendliness have endeared Ted to thousands of fly fishers who have happened to pass through the town of Dunsmuir. Ted has found that his unique fly patterns and techniques work as well in the East as they do in freestone streams of the West.

When you become efficient in controlling line and detecting strikes in this short-line method, you are ready to attempt the same with longer casts and techniques as described in Chapter 10. The additional lengths of line coupled with increased terminal weight make long-line, up-stream nymphing one of the most difficult fly fishing methods to master.

Selected References

Green, L. "Nymphs Plain and Simple," *Field & Stream*, 1973, February.
Green, L. "Ted Fay's Deadly Wet Fly Concept," *Angler*, 1975, November-December.

Humphreys, J. *Joe Humphreys's Trout Tactics*. Harrisburg, Pa: Stackpole, 1981.

La Fontaine, G. "The Misunderstood Caddis Pupa," in Scientific Angler (Ed), *Fly Fishing Handbook*. Point Pleasant, N.J.: Aqua-Field, 1980.

Scott, J. "The Leisenring Lift," *Flyfishing the West*, 1979, November-December.

8
UP AND ACROSS STREAM DRY FLY FISHING
Beyond Pocket Water

The Fishing Situation

The fishing techniques described in this chapter constitute what may be considered the "classic" method of fly fishing. It is easily the most popular method.

Though the fundamentals of upstream, dry fly fishing are frequently learned in pocket water with the short-line techniques described in Chapter 4, most flyrodders associate dry fly fishing with longer pools and runs. Thus one envisions casts of 25 feet or more falling on moderately-flowing riffles, quiet glides, or the long, narrow pools of small streams. The common ingredients of these water types are the presence of 1) relatively even water flow in which to lay out line, leader and fly, and 2) relatively shallow water (eg., between 1 and 4 feet) through which trout can easily rise to surface food.

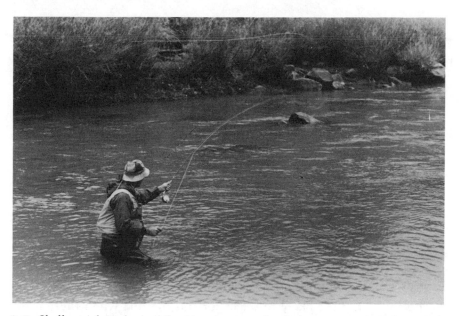

8-1: *Shallow, relatively even-flowing water provides the opportunity to reach out with a dry fly.*

Perhaps the most difficult problem you experience in learning this method is that of handling long lengths of upstream-cast line for the first time. This particular line-control problem becomes most evident in the faster runs. However, the pleasure of laying out line in a delicate cast, the fascination of watching a dry fly bobbing toward you in the currents, and the thrill of a surface strike explain why so many people enjoy this form of fishing.

Rigging Adaptations

In this method there is no need to depart from the general-purpose fly rod, reel, and floating line suggested in Chapter 1. Nine-foot leaders are popular in long pools, often tapered down to 4X or 5X and used with size 14 dry flies. Toward the end of the day, however, you may choose to switch to a larger fly as light fades. Reduced light intensity and the increased insect activity associated with it, often make the trout less cautious.

8-2: *Swept-back hair wings of the Elk Hair Caddis give the downwing profile of adult caddisflies (top) and stoneflies (bottom).*

The fly I am most likely to select for this method when there is no apparent hatch to match is a size 14 Elk Hair Caddis as designed by Al Troth of Dillon, Montana. It is a good general-purpose attractor that floats well and provides a convincing silhouette of downwing insects, including some terrestrials, stoneflies and, of course, caddisflies. I always try to keep a stock of this pattern in various sizes from 12 to 18 and tied both with dark and light elk hair.

In particularly quiet pools, 12-foot leaders provide a little extra distance between your fly and the relatively thick, visible fly line. Such water is more transparent so small tippets (e.g., 5X or 6X) and flies (e.g., size 16) will help fool trout that have extra time to scrutinize your offerings.

Fast-water favorite, the hackled peacock is "near enough" to various dark insects when trout feed generally. Moving clockwise from top, insects are mayfly nymph, carpenter ant, alderfly, terrestrial fly, alderfly larva, beetle, cased caddisfly larva, and creek damselfly nymph.

Leisenring Spider fills the bill when a light-toned sunken fly is needed in mixed currents. Clockwise from top are cranefly, mayfly, stonefly, caddisfly, caddisfly pupa, and caddisfly larva.

Sunken-fly pyramid reveals transition from "impressionistic" fast water flies on the right to "imitative" slow water flies on left (e.g., specific imitations of mayfly nymph (top), caddisfly pupae, and caddisfly larva (bottom).

Fly tyer's concern for size, shape and color of insects
is evident in comparing artificial (i.e., Brooks' Montana
Stone) to natural stonefly nymph.

Sunkey-fly searching in slow water often starts with a Hare's Ear Nymph. Invertebrates it resembles include (from 1 o'clock) caddisfly larva, scud, swimming mayfly nymph, water boatman, and caddisfly pupa.

"Deep-water doubling" with Brooks' Assam Dragon. When wet (bottom right) it imitates a dragonfly nymph (pictured) or a small fish. When modified by leaving a strip of fur trailing behind (top), it doubles for baitfish or leech.

Sculpin sculpted from feather and fur by Dave Whitlock catches the essential shape of this widely-distributed forage fish.

General-purpose dry flies (clockwise from 12 o'clock) include Irresistible, Elk Hair Caddis, Grizzly Wulff, Grizzly Spider, Orange Palmer, and Horner Deer Hair (Humpy).

The Approach

If you park close to the stream, it may be worth your while to collect insects from streamside foliage before fishing. Large sweep nets that are associated with collecting butterflies sometimes reveal the presence of heavy concentrations of terrestrials, such as carpenter ants, or of aquatic insects that have emerged recently. If you are unable to recognize the most common aquatic insects, at least you can select fly patterns that resemble those that are abundant on the foliage. An important part of this resemblance is the shape of the insect's wings. This wing shape also guides your learning of the most common insects. For example, the wings of an adult stonefly are folded back flat on its body. The wings of an adult caddisfly are also folded back—but in a roof or tent shape. Both are thought of as downwing flies in contrast to the mayfly duns, whose wings are upright at rest—like the sails of a sailboat. To speed up your learning of these insects, you can collect them in a small, water-tight bottle or film container and take them to your local fly-shop proprietor for identification.

In both pocket-water methods, I have suggested an upstream-wading, upstream-casting approach. This approach also works on the longer pools envisioned here, though concealment is achieved by staying farther back from the fish and casting more line.

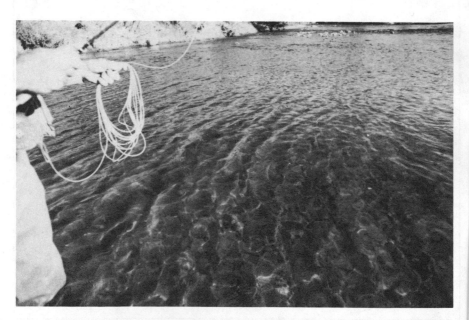

8-3: *Retrieving line into coils saves time when you need to wade 15 or 20 steps upstream between casts.*

You should look for casting positions with relatively even flow upstream on which to drift the line, leader and fly. In such unbroken water you frequently have a choice of upstream casting angles, though a cast dropped directly upstream may "line the trout"—that is, place the fly line close enough over the fish to spook it.

A careless habit that you can pick up in fishing this method is to cast continuously while wading upstream. One consequence is to miss fish that strike when you are stumbling or concentrating on wading. Another is to trip and fall while watching the fly.

When you have to wade more than a few steps and are rigged with a leader not longer than nine feet, you can stop fishing by retrieving line in large coils with the fly left hanging above the level of the water (to stay dry). After wading to the next casting position, the coiled line can be dropped to the water and the line extended by false casting. With feet planted, you are than able to concentrate on fishing. This doesn't work with 12-foot leaders because with only leader beyond the rod tip, the line will slide back through the guides.

Casting Techniques

8-4: *A fly's soft, fluttery drop to the water is achieved with a lowered backcast and raised forecast.*

The overhead cast remains the bread-and-butter cast of this method, though its plane is tilted backward whenever you wish to soften the drop of your fly to the water. I also use this concept of lowering the backcast and raising the forecast to achieve a vertical, fluttering drop much like the egg-laying flight of various aquatic insects. In fact this is an excellent cast to use with an Elk Hair Caddis whenever small caddisflies or stoneflies can be seen egg-laying.

A specialty cast that I use frequently when fishing this method is a curve cast. Throwing an upstream curve in a cast that has been delivered up and across stream reduces the possibility of having the leader drift over the fish ahead of the fly, (which can spook fish in quiet water). Having the line positioned on the water a little farther upstream than when straight also helps delay the onset of drag in tricky currents. To be effective, the curve should appear throughout the entire leader, something that becomes difficult to accomplish in leaders longer than about nine feet.

The curve cast, however it is taught, is based on the principle that the line goes where the rod tip sends it. Understanding this principle seems to speed up the learning of this cast for many beginners. I have them start the hand and rod moving toward their target at the beginning of the forward cast and, as quickly as possible, move the tip to one side or another. Typically, the farthest part of the line and the leader land

8-5: *Curve casting under overhanging foliage requires an over-powered sidearm delivery.*

pointing to the target, and a sharp angle in the line near the rod indicates where the tip was moved to the side. With practice, the rod tip movements are made quicker and smoother to form a gentle curve in the leader and line closer to the fly.

8-6: *Over-powering the off-side cast enables you to achieve a negative curve (i.e., curve to the left for a left-handed caster).*

Eventually you may want to learn curve casts with the rod tip canted down to either side to slide the fly under overhanging foliage. This variation involves some overpowering so that the sideways loop not only straightens but reverses its curve before being dropped to the surface. If you are a right-handed caster facing upstream, you can use this "positive" curve cast to reach fish lying close to the bank off to your left. To accomplish this cast when the fish and bank are off to your right, you can tilt the rod over your head so that the tip is over your left shoulder. This "off side" cast is also overpowered to produce an upstream curve.

Line-Handling and Fishing Techniques

"Fishing the rise" is one of the traditional elements of upstream dry fly fishing. In some privately-controlled English streams, for example, you are allowed to cast only to rising fish. In such fishing you learn to present the fly slightly off to your side of the trout to keep the line and leader from drifting over it.

Fishing the rise is not always possible. You may know streams, such as the UPper Sacramento River, where there are days when trout are seldom seen rising yet will take a dry fly readily. Wating for a fish to rise would only waste valuable fishing time. In a stream such as this, you get more action by "fishing the water"—fishing progressively upstream through likely looking runs.

8-7: *Faint current tongues on the right reveal several drift lanes that are slow enough to be fished from the same spot before wading farther upstream.*

With years of experience, you begin to know where in the pool the fish is most likely to rise and to which cast. I demonstrated this one day to Bob Dering, one of the capable fly fishermen who helps me teach classes on the Upper Sacramento. On this particular day, I wanted to get a photograph of a trout taking a dry fly, and soon came within view of a riffle that "couldn't miss." Bob was skeptical but took the camera, listened to my instructions for taking the picture, and crawled into position close to where I told him the fish would rise. After snapping the shutter, Bob's outcry was of such an irritated nature that I thought he had missed the shot. I was wrong. "Not only did you predict that a trout would rise, where it would rise, to which cast, and that you would hook it, but you predicted that I would get the picture," he exclaimed. Mostly Bob was annoyed that I had predicted his behavior. Undoubtedly I was a little lucky, though experience minimizes much of the guesswork. I had never fished that run before.

Though the upper reaches of a particular riffle may look to be the most promising water, the experienced upstream dry fly fisher learns to cover the downstream portions first, especially in clear, shallow pools where fish are easily spooked. When you cast to the downstream water first, fish startled by the landing of the fly or leader are likely to move to nearby cover without alarming the better fish farther upstream. However, when you attempt to by-pass the tail of the pool, these same fish are apt to be startled by your silhouette or the fly line and are likely to bolt upstream in panic, thus "putting down" any fish feeding there.

When fishing up through a riffle, you typically move in stages, taking a few steps, then making a few casts. Your casts from a single location may sample several drift lanes and distances (through extending line). On each cast the fly is gently lifted off the water far enough upstream to keep any fish that have followed the fly from seeing you.

In slow-moving runs I sometimes gather in line by means of an old technique call the hand-twist retrieve which you may read about elsewhere. I don't emphasize its use in my teaching, because stripping in line from behind the rod hand is easier for beginners to learn and controls line better in fast currents, which makes it a more versatile technique.

Hooking and Landing the Fish

Forty feet of line or more drifting on the water upstream of you usually forms some slack despite your best line-handling efforts. This being the case, your movements in setting the hook must be extensive enough to straighten the line as well as to move the fly. The more slack line that is on the water, the more extensive these movements must be. Once again I recommend that you set the hook by pulling the line to your left (and down) while moving the rod up and to your right (if you are right handed). These movements can be lengthened when necessary to drive the hook home.

When I have hooked a good fish well upstream of me, I try to keep rod pressure on it in the hope that it will move away from this resistance—farther upstream. If this happens, the trout is moving against the force of the current as well as against the resistance in the fly rod and will soon tire itself. It should be brought to net quickly so it doesn't become overly exhausted. Then it will have an excellent chance to survive when you release it.

If your trout jumps, and you have the presence of mind to think of it, you should lower the rod. This has the effect of giving a little line at a time when the trout's movement into the air may have added to the strain on the leader. Giving this line may also prevent the tippet from breaking if the fish should land on it.

Wading and Safety

In a previous chaptr I mentioned the preferred "crab-like" shuffling movements you should use when wading upstream. With a wading staff, you have the addition of a third "foot." In using these three wading feet, it is important to remember that two of them should always provide firm support while the other moves. I have slipped with a wading staff and realized it was almost always because I had been moving the staff and one of my feet at the same time. With rare exception, your wading staff should be held on your upstream side. If you depend on the support of a staff held on your downstream side, you risk a disorienting head-downstream fall.

My staff is an old bamboo ski pole with the ring removed from the bottom. Occasionally I have used a head limb for this purpose when making an unexpected crossing, but only after testing its strength by leaning hard against it.

Variations of this Method

The ability to fish this method effectively simplifies the learning of long-line, upstream nymphing as described in Chapter 10. Much of the approach, the casting angles, the wading, and the line-handling are the same.

Selected References

Fox, C. "Upstream, the Classic Presentation," in J. Migel (Ed.), *The Masters on the Dry Fly*. Philadelphia: Lippencott, 1977.

Goddard, J. and Clarke, B. *The Trout and the Fly*. Garden City, New York: Doubleday, 1980.

Marinaro, V. *A Modern Dry-Fly Code*. New York: Crown, 1970.

Schwiebert, E. "How I Fish Dry Flies," *Sports Afield*, 1974, February.

Sosin, M. "Brown Trout Breakthrough," *Sports Afield*, 1982, February.

Wilson D. *Fishing the Dry Fly*. London: A. & C. Black, 1970.

9
DOWN AND
ACROSS STREAM
DRY FLY FISHING
A Presentation for Educated
Meadow-Stream Trout

The Fishing Situation

Fishing a dry fish with a downstream-angled cast represents a departure from the dry fly theory and methods discussed thus far. This downstream dry fly method has become increasingly popular on some waters, most often on meadow streams inhabited by "educated" trout.

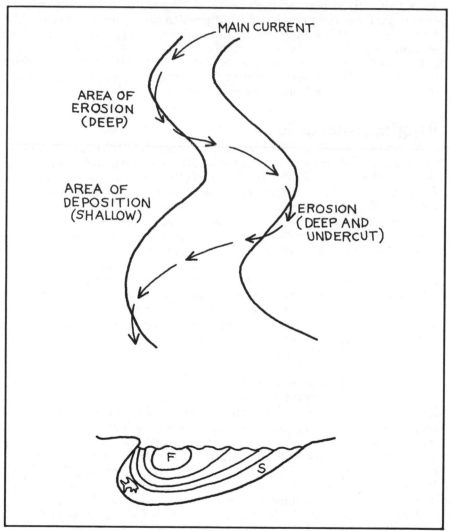

9-1: *Deep trout holds may be formed wherever the main current of a meandering stream swings to the bank. The cross-section of a typical undercut bank shows the location of fastest (F) and slowest currents (S).*

One of the problems that meadow-stream anglers face is how to catch trout that refuse to move out of extremely narrow feeding lanes, of only a few inches. Often your fly must be dropped directly upstream of such trout. As an upstream caster you can no longer present the fly off to one side but must move your cast in closer to the fish because of the accuracy required. This increases the likelihood that part of your leader will drift over the trout before the fly arrives. Unfortunately, such trout often become leader shy and learn to refuse this presentation. So there are times in which it pays to drift your fly down to the fish ahead of the leader—by quartering your cast down and across stream.

Sometimes this presentation is necessary to achieve a drag-free drift of your fly. This is most apparent when you cast to a big trout that has learned to rise in the midst of uneven currents.

Rigging Adaptations

At times you will want to be able to reach fish that are 50 feet or more away. This may be due to the width of a particular stream or to the fact that you and the trout are facing one another as you cast towards the fish from upstream. Though your general-purpose rod and number 6 DT fly line may do a satisfactory job in this situation, an increasing number of meadow-stream anglers are using delicate feeling, long, graphite rods. A 9-9½ foot graphite that casts a number 4 or 5 line may already be the standard on such streams.

The action you prefer in such a rod may be related to a specific feature or demand of this form of fishing. For example, if you have difficulty controlling your casting loops with 50 feet of line out, you could benefit from a rod with a relatively stiff butt action. On the other hand, you may prefer to have a rod that provides more shock absorption throughout its length for setting hooks and playing big fish on light tippets. This may lead you to select a rod with a relatively "soft" butt.

If you fish this method with abbreviated double hauls you may prefer to use a weight-forward fly line. Short "tugs" or hauls with the line hand increase the speed of the line in the air and thus contribute to loop control (by shortening the time during which a line may collapse on itself). Also you will find that a weight-forward line makes it easier for you to feed or shake line out through the guides when extending a drift. (This concept will be covered in the section on Line-Handling). However, some dry fly anglers believe the fly is presented more delicately with double-tapered lines and use them exclusively.

A typical leader for down and across dry fly fishing is about 12 feet long with a tippet of 5X or 6X. The tippet section may be unusually long—sometimes three to six feet in length. This extra length of fine tippet delays drag and provides extra stretch to the leader. You may want to consider using as small or fine a tippet diameter as conditions permit. Surprisingly big fish are taken on 6X or 7X tippets—if the material is in good condition. You should always pull the ends of a piece of tippet material before attaching it or somehow test to make sure it hasn't started to deteriorate and lose strength.

This strong new tippet material (e.g., Aeon or C.S.E. brands) holds better with the improved surgeon's knot than with the traditional blood knot. Additional strength can also be achieved at the fly itself by using a variation of the clinch knot in which the tag end of the tippet is inserted through the hook eye twice.

The standard or traditional dry fly patterns are not always preferred on meadow streams, as too much hackle sticking down through the surface film is thought to be unrealistic in relation to the indentations made by an insect's legs. Two of my favorite tying variations are the Paradun and Comparadun patterns. Of the two, the Paradun sits a little lower in the water and may be more effective when fish are feeding on various stages of mayflies that are down in the surface film (e.g., emerging nymph, spinner). On the other hand, the Comparadun is extremely durable and continues to float well after several fish have been taken in quick succession.

The Approach

"Mountain stream" anglers, when first exposed to a meadow stream, typically rig their fly rods and begin casting immediately. This can be a great mistake. Meadow streams give you the opportunity to learn by watching fish. Before rigging up, you should stay well back from shore, find an elevated bank with suitable light conditions, and don your polarized glasses and hat (with black under the brim), to see trout holding among weedbeds. The most skilled anglers in some of our best meadow streams will sometimes observe for several hours until they find a trout that is large enough to offer a sufficient challenge to their skills. They choose not to fish the water, preferring to spend their time casting to one, visible trout.

When you have watched enough to analyze the situation, it is time to rig up and move quietly to a spot well upstream of the fish. You should also resist the "mountain stream" angler's tendency to wade, unless it is necessary to get the particular drift you want. The higher position on the bank affords a better view of your drifting fly and leader, and any drag problems that might develop. If you have to wade, check to make sure your movements are slow enough that you can't see water being pushed ahead of you. Differences in water pressure are transmitted far and quickly in quiet, unbroken water.

As you move toward your trout from well upstream and off to one side, you should be aware of the trout's "window" or "cone of vision," which is explained in Marinaro's *The Ring in the Rise* and Goddard & Clarke's *The Trout and the Fly*. What you want to do is to present the fly a few feet directly upstream of this window, so it arrives ahead of the

9-2: *The trout's "window" to life above water leaves you 10 degrees within which to conceal yourself.*

leader. The location of the window is important because it marks the spot from which the trout can view objects above the water's surface. Your own silhouette must be low enough to fit within the first 10 degrees above horizontal (surface of the water), if you wish to remain concealed. Perhaps when descending a steep trail above a stream, you have already been impressed with how well a trout can detect your movements through clear, undisturbed water.

Casting Techniques

At times trout may be "put down" by your false casts. When this happens, you learn to adjust by extending line with false casts angled in a direction well off to one side of the fish.

Among the most useful specialized casts in this type of fishing is an old technique that has recently been popularized as the "reach cast." This cast enables you to place the fly line on the water at a different angle than with a standard, overhead cast. Its most common application is in placing the line farther upstream on the water—as if cast by someone standing several feet to your upstream side. This effect is accomplished by moving your casting hand and the fly rod steadily off to one side after you have applied the initial power to the forward cast.

You begin fishing this cast with the tip of your fly rod "reached" upstream. Throughout the drift, the tip is moved steadily downstream to allow the line and fly to drift naturally until the tip is "reached"

9-3: *Completing the reach cast with rod extended to the upstream side has positioned the line well upstream of a fly being drifted off to the left.*

downstream before lifting the fly off the water. This movement of the rod tip extends the drag-free drift.

A line that is cast down and across stream falls to the water, moves away from you, straightens, and in so doing, makes your fly drag unnaturally. The fact that this can all happen within a very few seconds underlines the need for slack in your line to delay the onset of drag. Most downstream dry fly anglers develop several slack-line casts for different situations.

Perhaps the most generally useful one is the "dry fly shock cast" because it puts the slack in the leader near the fly. When line has been cast more across stream than down, and is drifting on currents moving at different speeds, the slack in the leader conceals (for a short time) the fact that some of the line has overtaken the fly enough to be pulling on the rest of the drifting line.

This leader slack is achieved by aiming the forecast slightly upward, overpowering it, and making a high, abrupt stop. The overpowered line is "shocked" as it straightens above the water, and the leader recoils or bounces back toward the line. At this time the rod tip is dropped so the line falls to the water before any of the slack can be lost.

Sometimes the slack is intentionally put into the line itself. In general, this works best when casting more downstream than across stream. The serpentine or "S" cast is the most common example. The cast is aimed high, and the rod tip moved from side to side throughout

9-4: *Side-to-side movements of the rod during the serpentine cast put "S" curves in the airborne line.*

the delivery so the line falls to the water in alternating curves. The draw-back cast is a more useful variation for putting slack in the line. Drawing the fly rod back toward you before the fly hits the water produces slack in the line near the fly rod. This slack becomes available for extending the drift. If your fly is cast beyond a trout's feeding lane, you can draw it back onto the water directly upstream of the trout's lie. This feature makes the cast popular with boat guides, who are paid to produce fish for some rather inept casters.

The best slack-line casts for particular pools are sometimes combinations of basic techniques. My favorite is one that Frank Collin and I put together one August day on Hat Creek, the popular meadow stream near Burney, California. Frank is very analytical and quite skilled as a fly fisher and fly tyer.

We were trying to get as long a drag-free drift as possible in slow water beyond the fast currents our line had to drift in. Our best drifts were achieved by combining five elements: 1) extra long tippets (5 to 6 feet); 2) low back cast and high forward "pile cast"; 3) release of line during the forward cast; 4) early dropping of the rod tip; and 4) a mending of the line before the fly hit the water. We laughingly refer to this particular combination as a "Ray Guy" cast because the fly has a five-second "hang time" in the air, like so many of the famous punter's best kicks.

9-5: *Slack line on the water near the rod is achieved with a draw-back cast. As the line straightens in the air on your forward cast, pull the rod (and the line) back toward you (1). Then drop the rod tip low (2) to place the slack on the water. In a downstream presentation, the fly can drift naturally until the last of this slack line has straightened.*

Line-Handling and Fishing Techniques

One of the fascinating things about this kind of fishing is analyzing currents to decide what adjustments to make in casting position, cast, and line-handling to achieve a drag-free drift.

A common error people make, in my estimation, is to cast over the fish without first checking the drift and making some adjustments. I see people put down trout with their very first presentation because of unanticipated drag. Often they are fishing a much longer cast than the situation requires. Some years back, Andre Puyans, the internationally known fly fisherman and fly tyer, introduced me to the concept of an "imaginary grid" on the surface of the water. This grid is envisioned as an aid in remembering to move your fly systematically closer to the fish with each cast. Your first casts should fall far short of the fish—too far to draw strikes or rejections. However, they enable you to observe the way your fly is drifting. As you cast the fly closer to the fish, you are making adjustments in casting angle, line length, and type of cast until you are satisfied with the drift. Then, instead of extending more line, your final adjustments onto the fish are made by moving closer to it (when conditions permit). So your own position, rather than line length, is varied when finally moving "on to the fish."

A common form of line-handling on many meadow streams is "feeding" line into the drift. Feeding a controlled amount of line extends the drift to fish that are exceptionally wary or simply beyond casting range downstream. Feeding line is accomplished by lowering the rod tip and flipping it up and down. It is an action somewhat like mending line upstream while using the line hand to pay line out through the guides (from the surplus line dropping from the reel). The small diameter of the middle section of a weight-forward line feeds down through the guides more readily than does a thicker double-tapered line.

Of course the fly must then be brought back toward you without pulling the line, leader, and fly over the fish. To do this you hold the rod to the side away from the trout. This consumes time and soaks the fly. If I must feed line in this way and want to watch my fly for drag, I first select a buoyant pattern, such as a small Humpy or Comparadun, and hope it does the job.

Mending line also has a place in downstream dry fly fishing, though some anglers believe you can't mend without also moving your fly. Most commonly I use the mend when the line close to me is drifting much faster than the fly itself farther out. If you use a long leader and your fly has been drifting a couple of seconds it is not difficult to mend line without moving the fly. And several mends might be required to achieve the drift you want.

Hooking and Landing the Trout

Successfully hooking a trout that is downstream of you can be a tricky business. In effect, you are pulling the fly back upstream, out of the fish's mouth, rather than setting it into the side of the jaw as you often do when downstream of the fish. The combination of fine tippets, hooks with small gapes, and very large trout can result in many fish being lost at the moment of the take.

As indicated previously, you may want to select a flyrod with this moment in mind, choosing one that is soft enough to be forgiving when excessive force is applied in reaction to a sudden strike.

Sometimes a trout takes your fly when the line is on the water in a long curve. If you set the hook by raising the rod in this situation, you encounter considerable resistance of surface tension on your line. Your movement will be transmitted to the fly quicker if it is made with the rod parallel to the surface and away from the fly line.

In playing a fish that is pulling downstream away from you, your main concern should be to minimize the pressure or resistance against it and your tippet. (When the fish stops using energy, then is the time for you to increase pressure.) One thing you can do is to hold your rod high to keep as much line in the air as possible, since line on the water increases the resistance and thus adds to the pressure on the tippet.

Lowering your rod tip and pointing the rod directly toward the fish helps the line slide through the guides with a minimum of resistance. Both of these concepts can be incorporated into a single technique by holding the rod hand high, but keeping the rod in a more horizontal than vertical angle.

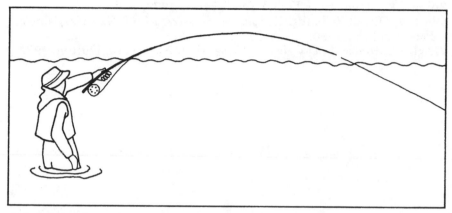

9-6: *Minimizing resistance against a running fish means holding the rod high (to keep line off the water) and horizontal (to let line slip through the guides).*

I realize there are times when you will want to apply more pressure to a downstream-pulling fish, such as when you can't follow it farther downstream.

Wading and Safety
Even when not wading, safety should be on your mind. In walking the bank of a meadow stream, you should anticipate the presence of undercut banks whenever the main current is on your side, and expect beaver or muskrat tunnels to be underfoot. The high grass on the banks of these streams often conceals holes or soft footing. These are all reasons for walking carefully and testing the footing constantly. It is not a place to be in a hurry.

Variations of this Method
Although not discussed here, many dry fly anglers fish downstream angles on the mixed currents of mountain streams. Leonard Wright's variation of twitching the downstream-cast dry fly to imitate the upstream surge of an egg-laying caddisfly is a specialized application of this general method.

Selected References
Arbona, F. *Mayflies, the Angler and the Trout.* Tulsa, Oklahoma: Winchester Press, 1980.

Caucci, A. and Nastasi, B. *Hatches*. Woodside, New York: Comparahatch, 1975.

Harrop, R. "Meadow Streams—The Ultimate Challenge," in Scientific Anglers (Ed.), *Fly Fishing Handbook*. Point Pleasant, New Jersey: Aqua-Field, 1980.

Marinaro, V. *In the Ring of the Rise*, New York: Crown, 1976.

Robins, K. "Nymph or Dun," *The Flyfisher*. 1979, Fall.

Swisher, D. and Richards, C. *Tying the Swisher/Richards Flies*. Harrisburg, Pa: Stackpole, 1980.

Wright, L. *Fishing the Dry Fly as a Living Insect*. New York: Dutton, 1972.

10
UPSTREAM NYMPHING
Further Challenges
In Line Control, Naturalness and Depth

The Fishing Situation

One of my greatest pleasures in fly fishing is experimenting with different techniques or variations. Yet, if I had to limit myself to one method, there would be no hesitation in making my choice. I would fish a nymph with the line laid out on the water upstream of me. In some respects this type of fishing is an extension of the short-line, sunken-fly method described earlier. It is different in that there is more line being fished, and that the line is floating on the water, rather than cutting directly through it.

This upstream, line-on-the-water method of nymphing owes part of its appeal to the fact that it is also similar to upstream, dry fly fishing, at least in the approach, the casting, and much of the line handling. It has long been recognized as the most palatable alternative for the dry fly angler who is forced to sink the fly to attract trout. I had to learn from experience that some of the best fish in moving water seldom feed near the surface. I mentally kick myself everytime I think of how many decent-sized trout I fished over unknowingly during the 1940s and 50s—when I fished only with dry flies.

For me, much of the pleasure in this method is in the subtlety of strike detection, particularly when the first indication of a trout's take is something less than an obvious dip, jerk, or stop in my leader. Maintaining enough line control to detect at least some of the subtle takes in various types of water is challenge enough for any angler.

The adaptability of upstream nymphing to many different types of water also adds to the appeal of this method. The terminal rigging, in particular, can be altered in a number of ways to accommodate the need for line control, depth, and naturalness in stretches of water that are quite different from one another.

The earliest application of this method may have been in gently-flowing streams of England. In a book published in 1939, *Nymph Fishing for Chalk Stream Trout*, Skues recounted how he started using this method to stalk individual, visible trout years before. This method is equally effective in a wide assortment of mountain-stream riffles and pools, where "fishing the water" makes more sense.

This type of fishing seems least appropriate in very fast runs (e.g., rapids, fast riffles and glides) and in very short runs (e.g., cascades, pocket water). I have already described methods that are better suited to such water.

Rigging Adaptations

Fly rods used for upstream nymphing are as varied as the water itself. Where the method is used to cast substantial weight in rough water, you may want a rod that casts a number 7 line, but where it is used to cast small nymphs in quiet flow, you may prefer one that casts a number 5 line. Our general-purpose rod is adequate in both situations.

Though I own a few sink-tip lines, I invariably use floating lines in this method. If I am casting much terminal weight (e.g., one or two number 7 split shot) a distance of 40 to 50 feet, I use a double-tapered line rather than a weight-forward. The extra weight in the larger diameter behind the first 30 feet handles the casting of leader weight better than the thinner weight-forward line.

As I have stated, much of the adaptability of this method comes through adjusting the terminal tackle to "match the water." This may be done by varying a) the length and tippet diameter of the leader, b) the placement and quantity of leader weight, c) the type and placement of a "strike indicator" (if used), and d) the number, weight, size, and pattern of flies.

It might be of value here to describe several of the most distinctive riggings that are used in upstream nymphing. First, the one that is most similar to dry fly fishing involves little more than replacing the dry fly with a lightly-weighted nymph. The leader butt is usually greased with flotant to facilitate strike detection in the shallow, quiet pools where this variation is typically used.

In my teaching, I have noticed that some experienced dry fly anglers have difficulty shifting their concentration from a fly they can no longer see (but still look for) to the visible part of the leader. The addition of a more obvious "strike indicator" serves to focus their attention while they become accustomed to this method. Though a wide variety of materials are used for thie flyfisher's "bobber," I most often attach to my leader a small red piece of the best floating synthetic yarn I can get my hands on, trimming it into a small ball of about 1/8th of an inch in diameter. Near dark I have been known to use a Troth Caddis on a short dropper as my indicator. This indicator outfishes my nymph at times. Mostly, however, I prefer not to use an indicator. I use one when the distance of a cast, or the shade, glare, or chop on the water makes seeing my leader difficult.

In quiet water, the placement of the indicator becomes critical, because the trout often pick up the nymph without moving very far or very fast. To detect such quiet takes, the indicator must be as close to the fly as possible while still providing enough tippet length to get the fly down near the trout's feeding level. This is accomplished with a rather vertical drop of the fly, using as much weight as you can without sinking the indicator. Two California anglers, Bob Howe and Dave Hixon, have fine-tuned this particular theory of rigging to take some huge brown trout from quiet-flowing rivers in that state.

A very different rigging may be called for on big, freestone streams where depth and current speed vary considerably from pool to pool. The most extreme adjustments are made by changing leader length. This can be done quickly when the leader butt has been connected to the tippet by loops, as publicized by Lefty Kreh. In my particular adaptation of this loop system, the permanent leader butt is 5½-feet long, and my pre-tied tippets allow me to fish leaders from 7 to 12-feet long. With the interconnecting loops, the only knots you need to tie on the stream are those at the fly itself.

Most of the time such extreme changes in leader length are not necessary, and you can stay with a leader of about nine feet. One much shorter than this sometimes gets the fly line too close to the line on upstream casts or fails to give you adequate depth from the floating line. A leader much longer than nine feet becomes more difficult to cast with weight (particularly when trees line the banks) and is more difficult to control in the water where currents are mixed. When

10-1: *"Realism" in fly patterns gains importance in quiet water where trout have time to inspect their food. André Puyan's AP nymphs are realistic enough to imitate mayfly nymphs in slow water yet general enough to pass for either stonefly nymphs (top) or mayfly nymphs (bottom) where currents are faster. The distinguishing feature between these two nymphs is the presence of gills on the mayfly's abdomen.*

fishing this leader, you can still make adjustments to variations in depth and current speed by changing the size or number of removable split shot on the leader. The quickness with which this form of leader weight can be added or removed is its most important characteristic, because you might change weight two or three times in the same run.

The exact placement of the weight may have a pronounced effect on how naturally your fly sinks, and how many strikes come while it is sinking. When all the weight is concentrated in one place, that part of the leader plummets to the bottom. Trout are seldom attracted to a fly that is sinking this fast. Through pool-testing a two-fly rigging, we found that heavy weight sinks more naturally when most of it is placed in two locations—on the leader just above the dropper strand and on the tail fly (end fly).

This rigging, with two weighted flies and split shot, works well when nymphing in big, mountain streams. Flies we have discussed previously, such as a Leisenring Spider, Hare's Ear Nymph, Gray-Hackle Peacock, or dark A.P. Nymph, work well on the dropper fly in about size 10. I usually use something larger on the tail fly, such as a number 6 or 8 golden-stonefly nymph. Frank Collin and I developed the pattern we prefer, the C.K. Perlid, which was published in the May-June 1981 issue of *Flyfishing the West.*

If the trout show a preference for one fly, I switch the other for a pattern closer to the one that is working. In this way I try to zero-in on a specific feeding tendency as early as possible, if one exists. My friend, Dick Holland, once took two fifteen-inch brown trout from the same spot in quick succession and found that the one that grabbed his scud imitation was feeding on scuds, while the one that grabbed his caddis larva pattern was eating only caddis larva. This may not be the rule, but it happens.

The Approach

When "fishing the water" with this method, your approach is basically the same as when fishing up and across stream with a dry fly. Again, you position yourself where you are best able to lay the line and fly on relatively even-flowing water. Concealment is not as critical, however, when fishing to bottom-holding trout under a turbulent water surface.

When conditions permit you to spot individual trout, you spend a few moments observing its feeding behavior before attempting the first cast. In such gentle flow, you may want to position yourself to cast as much across stream as upstream in order to see the trout as clearly as possible when the fly approaches it.

The most fascinating part of the approach is looking at the water to decide how you will fish it. The more experienced and versatile you are, the more options you have. Sometimes, I force myself to "read the water " out loud—where the currents converge, where there is cover, where the fish should be, what is unusual. By doing this I often become aware of something subtle that I would have overlooked by reading the water unconsciously. This is important late in the season when hordes of anglers have worked over the obvious spots. Then you should read the water for something the others have missed, approach it from a different side, or use a different fishing technique.

Casting Techniques

Some of the casts I have mentioned previously, including the reach, roll, and curve casts, can be used when terminal weight isn't excessive. Casting problems arise when split shot or heavy flies are needed to achieve depth in rough water. You have already been advised to cant the rod off to the side and use large loops to cast weight safely.

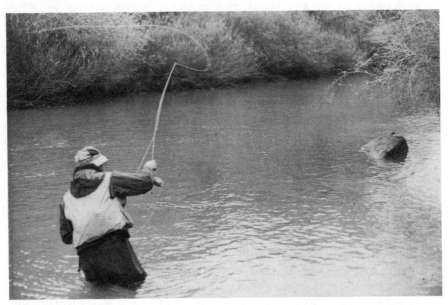

10-2: *Lowered left hip and outward-thrust elbow help tilt the rod for an off-side cast. Though the line has passed on the angler's left, note that the casting hand stays on his right.*

One casting variation that is useful whether leader weight is applied or not is the "off-side cast" alluded to in other chapters. This is the cast where you try to move the fly and line back and forth on your non-casting side (your left side, if a right handed caster). In wadable freestone rivers, the streamside alders or willows may force you to spend much of the day using this technique, which is sometimes referred to as casting "off your left shoulder" or the "tilted plane cast." Mel Krieger has used these terms rather than "backhand cast" because

10-3: *Cast completed, the angler prepares to fish a drift close to a protected lie. Over-powering the next off-side cast would produce a curve around the upstream side of the rock.*

it is a different technique. Mel stresses keeping your casting hand on the right side, where it can apply power most effectively, whereas the backhand cast brings the casting hand over to the left side of your body. In the off-side cast the right elbow is moved away from the body in order that your forearm can stay aligned with the rod in being canted to the left.

This power emphasis becomes extremely important if you use the cast as I do in delivering splitshot 45 feet or more upstream on the off-side. With experienced timing and a wide arc, the fly can be dropped with surprisingly little splash. Many anglers don't realize that 45 feet of fly line represents enough weight to sharply reduce any disruptive effect that leader weight has on casting.

If you don't trust yourself with the off-side cast, you can always resort to the old technique of turning to face downstream, and reversing the casting strokes. In other words, you direct a forward cast downstream (as your backcast) and then deliver the fly upstream and onto the water with a backcast (used as your forward cast). This technique eliminates the need to cast off your left side, especially when learning to handle terminal weight. This technique is also useful when a wind flows hard from your casting side as it often does on lakes. One such day on Lake Pyramid in Nevada, I caught a seven pound cutthroat with this cast.

10-4: *Reversing your casting strokes is useful when foliage or wind make normal casting difficult. Though the angler here wants to cast upstream away from the camera, he has turned downstream to backcast with a forward casting motion.*

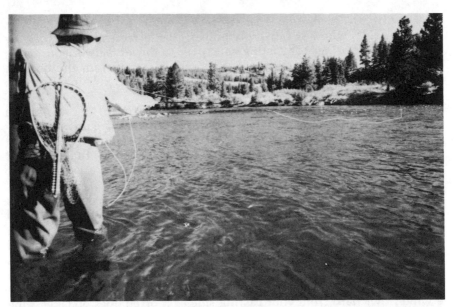

10-5: *Now he has delivered the fly back upstream onto the water with a backcasting motion and is pivoting in that direction to fish.*

Split shot becomes more difficult to cast when less line is used. It may become necessary to use the tension cast described in Chapter 5, where the friction of the water bends the rod to deliver the line upstream safely. The roll cast can also be used effectively with split shot as long as the leader weight is near the surface when the cast is made.

Line-Handling and Fishing Techniques

The interplay between depth, naturalness, and line-control sometimes means one is emphasized at the expense of another. Each pool is different, and the first few drifts will tell you if adjustments are needed to provide additional depth or perhaps better line control. Sometimes such adjustments can be made by varying the cast to present the fly and leader differently, without having to make alternations in your rigging.

If, for example, you need more depth early in the drift, you could use a tuck cast as mentioned in Chapter 7, or use any casting variation that puts slack in your leader. When you use a fine tippet and present it in loose coils, resistance to the fly's sinking is at a minimum.

10-6: *Constant stripping of line becomes a way of life for those who nymph upstream in fast water.*

However, there are other times when control of the line becomes more important than depth or naturalness. You need a drift that starts with as straight a leader as possible if the trout are hitting early in the drift, or tentatively in general, or when the submerged leader is developing excessive slack during the drift. A well-executed roll cast is one way of achieving this presentation with very little splash near the fly.

After the cast, the rod is sometimes manipulated for line-handling purposes. A "roll mend" is a useful technique when you cast a nymph up and across stream to a slot of slow water that lies beyond fast currents. As the fly begins to sink immediately after the cast, you cant the rod to the downstream side and make a sideward roll cast upstream that affects only the line that hasn't already started to sink. If done correctly, a little line rolls out and falls on the upstream side of the sinking leader. Perhaps more important is the fact that this maneuver can be repeated several times in quick succession to keep line from settling into fast currents between you and the fly. When the fly has drifted closer to you, a high rod and extended arm take over in preventing the line from falling on the fast water.

Another distinctive use of the fly rod is to fish the drift with the rod tip held well off to one side, rather than being pointed upstream toward the fly. I have taught this as the "rod ahead" variation because the rod tip is directly ahead of the drifting fly. Without thinking about it you may have developed this tendency when guiding your fly through a drift lane that veers away to one side.

But I use this "rod ahead" variation primarily to fish any fly through a narrow, fast chute of water, such as between two large midstream

10-7: *Angling the rod to the side when fishing upstream into fast slots of water keeps the tip in line with the drifting fly. Split-shot is thus pulled directly downstream in this "rod ahead" variation.*

rocks. Some of the biggest fish I have taken from freestone streams have found a protected lie beneath a strip of fast water. Such fish get large because their hold is not visible from above and they cannot be taken by conventional fly fishing methods. They get by-passed by anglers who work the water regularly.

I fish such runs by casting almost straight upstream with more weight on the leader than usual—enough to lower the fly through fast water. Once this weight has cut through the fast currents, it becomes a liability due to its potential for hanging up on rubble or submerged snags on the stream's bottom. I try to avoid such hang-ups by keeping the leader in a somewhat horizontal plane and not letting the weight settle.

The rod held to the side with the tip low sets the horizontal plane of the leader, and constant stripping keeps the weight moving. I wouldn't worry if the fly is moving slightly faster than the current, because it could represent a natural, downstream movement of a minnow or large invertebrate. However, if your rod tip is too low, the line-leader junction (your indicator here) will sink from view.

During this time the non-casting hand is busy stripping in line to keep pace with the moving water, as in many other fly fishing methods. When the flow of water is fast and variable enough to require fast, long strips, strikes become difficult to detect.

Hooking and Landing the Fish

When looking for the trout's take, I typically watch the farthest visible part of the leader (or strike indicator) for any departure whatsoever from its steady downstream movement. The subtle indication that a trout has picked up the fly is usually a change in this rate of movement of the leader. Inexperienced eyes will not see it, and it accounts for what some writers refer to as the "mystique of nymphing."

One day on California's Hot Creek, I took 10 fish in an hour and a half while a stream biologist stood next to me watching my leader. He didn't detect a single strike, because none was as obvious as a sudden stop, dip, or jerk. The movement of the leader had continued, but at a changed rate. It is a detectable difference, not magic. If you are new to this form of fishing, you first learn to recognize the more obvious, sudden movements of the leader, which are usually decisive pickups by the fish.

The situation is different when you are fishing to trout you can see. When satisfied that your nymph has been cast upstream of the trout in its feeding lane, you watch the leader (or indicator) until it approaches the fish. At this moment you shift your vision to the trout itself, which in effect, becomes you "indicator." Any turn or lift in its position or flash of a white mouth should be interpreted as a pickup.

When watching for strikes, I prefer to use short strips to keep my line hand close to the rod. Thus I leave myself a long distance to pull the line when needed to remove slack in setting the hook. And, as mentioned before, I also move the rod away from the line pull.

When large split shot are used and the entire leader is submerged, the line-leader junction becomes the strike indicator. However, when any of the leader butt is visible either on or below the surface, I watch it to detect strikes because it provides an earlier and more pronounced indication.

10-8: *A horizontally-bent rod helps steer a hooked fish away from snags or obstructions.*

When playing a hooked fish, it isn't always in your best interest to hold the rod upright. When you want to lead a fish away from an obstacle or keep its head from moving freely above the surface, it pays to hold the rod to one side with a horizontal bend. However, if weedbeds are present or if the fish starts running, you should return the rod to its upright angle.

Wading and Safety

Like most anglers who wade upstream, I had to learn the hard way to plan ahead. Maybe you won't have to.

What may happen is that you spot an unusually good piece of water on the far side of the stream, and by bracing yourself against the current and carefully wading up and across the heavy water, you are able to reach it and fish. Only then do you realize you have a problem. You find there is no wadable return route except the one that brought you. Only now it involves a down and across stream wade through strong currents. You may have to continue facing upstream to keep yourself braced against the current, and painfully inch your way back downstream with what seems like a thousand backward steps. For a while, you are a prisoner of the river. The lesson you learn is if you can't see a return route before first wading into tough currents, don't go.

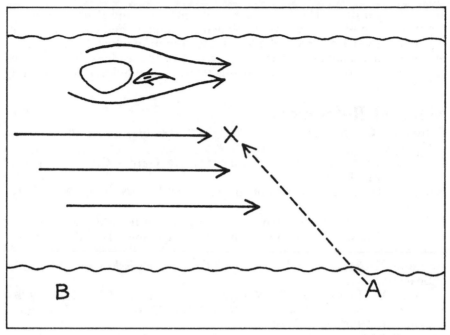

10-9: *Before a tough wade, such as the one drawn from A to X, check on a safe upstream "escape" such as the route from X to B.*

Variations of this Method

To some extent this chapter on upstream nymphing has been a discussion of variations. However, there is one variation that deserves special mention—a variation for big, deep, slow-moving "bait holes."

One spring day in the late 1960s, I was pool testing to confirm for myself that a 6-foot leader would sink a weighted fly faster than a 10-foot leader (other things being equal). For my own convenience, I had rigged the two rods with floating lines. Indeed, I found that my moderately-weighted fly sunk quicker on the shorter leader, but as I continued to watch, I saw the other fly eventually overtake it and sink deeper yet. I began to think of floating lines, long leaders, and slow, deep pools.

A week later, I had the opportunity to watch someone fish, who had already put this "program" or fishing variation together. Dick Holland, who has a reputation for taking exceptionally large fish from heavily fished waters, took ten fish between 14 and 24 inches using this method while the local fly fishing expert was doing well to catch that number in pocket water—but all under 14 inches.

In this variation you use as long a leader as necessary to get to the bottom and as much leader and fly weight as necessary to achieve a slow, natural drift. The fly is cast well upstream and fished carefully from the moment it lands. By the time it has approached you, the leader is dropping vertically from the line-leader junction which is held at the surface. Once again, any change in the rate of the leader's drift is likely to mean fish—often big, soft-hitting trout that wouldn't be felt on a sinking line.

Selected References

Fothergill, C. "Nymphing with Weight," *Fly Fisherman*, 1979, Season Opener.

Goddard, J. and Clarke, B. *The Trout and the Fly*. Garden City, New York: Doubleday, 1980.

Kreh, L. "Using the Loop Knot for Tippets," *Fly Fisherman*, 1979, Early Season.

Krieger, M. "The Tilted-Plane Cast," *Fly Fisherman*, 1981, March.

Kyte, A. "'Matching the Water' in Nymph Fishing," *Field & Stream* (in press).

Mingo, J. "Floating Nymphs on Spring Creeks," *Fly Fisherman*, 1980, Late Season.

Puyans, A. "Tying the A.P. Nymph Series," *Angler*, May-June, 1975.

Sawyer, F. *Nymphs and the Trout*. New York: Crown, 1973 (First published in 1958 by S. Paul).

Skues, G.E.M. *Nymph Fishing for Chalk Stream Trout*. London: A. & C. Black, 1939.

Whitlock, D. "Nymphs in 'Trouble Waters'," *Outdoor Life*, 1972, August.

11

A DEEP-NYMPH, FLOATING-LINE METHOD FOR LAKES

Sensitivity And Depth In Still Water

The Fishing Situation

Toward the end of the previous chapter I described a variation for nymphing deep in moving water with a floating line. A similar concept is gaining popularity in still water, particularly in lakes with extensive weedbeds or bottoms that harbor large numbers of small aquatic animals. These invertebrates—midge larva and pupa, mayfly nymphs, water boatmen, and small crustacians (scud)—are frequently vulnerable in large enough numbers that trout can feed while cruising deep, without having to make energy-expending rushes.

Based on this type of deep-feeding behavior, fly fishermen such as Brian Clarke of England and Hal Janssen of California have spent years refining concepts that have led to a lake method of fishing small, slow-moving nymphs with a floating line. This floating-line method features light, sensitive equipment and the imitation of small, aquatic insects, both of which contribute to its appeal to fly fishing anglers. When trout are feeding leisurely on small invertebrates, this floating line concept is preferred to sinking-line lake methods (described in Chapter 6), because the soft takes are transmitted to the surface far more readily along a light, thin leader than along a thick heavy flyline. By contrast, sinking line methods sometimes seem little more than dredging the bottom with large Wooly-Worms.

This floating line lake method, more than any other, is distinctive for its blending of sensitivity and depth.

Though the floating line concept has some attractive features, it would be a mistake to leave your sinking lines at home. They may be needed should a strong wind come up unexpectedly and push your floating line along the surface fast enough to interfere with your drift (and ability to detect strikes). And there's always the possibility that the trout will change their feeding pattern, necessitating your switch to a fast sinking line and a different fly, such as a leech pattern.

Rigging Adaptations

The link between a floating line and a nymph fished from between 5 and 15 feet deep is a very long leader, usually between 15 and 25 feet in length. Some fly rods handle the casting of such long leaders better than others. The fly rods that Hal Janssen has designed specifically for this method are slow action fiberglass rods with softness well down into the butt; they are between 8 and 8½ feet long and are unusually sensitive.

Presumably, the soft, slow-recovering rod applies power to the line over a longer period of time than a fast-action rod, with the result that energy gets transmitted farther down the leader (and more of it turns over).

On the basis of a little unscientific experimentation with a dozen fly rods and 25-foot leaders, I found that the casting advantage of my slow-action rods wasn't as clearcut over some of my other rods as I expected.

Most of my rods turned the long leaders over rather well. Perhaps the greatest advantage of the slow-action rod for this method is the amount of shock absorption it provides when you set the hook.

The general-purpose fly rod you own may or may not cast unusually long leaders well. Every fly rod performs differently. You may need to experiment to see what your rod can do with well-designed, long leaders. Possibly you will have to cut back a little to the 15 to 20-foot length to fish this method.

When 35 to 40 feet of fly line and an additional 25 feet of leader are to be cast, I prefer the smooth, controlled delivery of a good double-tapered line over a weight-forward. Probably a more important dimension of the line is its color. John Goddard is a quiet-water specialist from England who believes that the flash of a light-colored fly line overhead spooks trout in clear water below. Hal Janssen likes dark red because the dark shade minimizes this overhead flash while the red color is visible on the water.

The size of the line used is usually in the three to five weight range, so that you are using fly rods with enough sensitivity and lightness to handle small nymphs and 7X tippets.

I tie up my own knotted leaders for this method based on a "leader formula" developed by Hal Janssen. His tippets are long and fine, often down to 7X, so there is little restraint to the sinking of the fly. When I first tested one of his leaders, I was amazed how fast a size 16 weighted PT nymph can sink through the first few feet of still water.

With tippets in the 7X range and the possibility of large, strong trout, your terminal knots should be strong. I have already mentioned the variation of the clinch knot in which the end of the tippet is inserted twice through the eye of the hook. Some quiet water nymphers prefer a different knot, the duncan's loop. Its slip-knot feature is thought to give the nymph a little extra "swimming action." However, some people believe this knot breaks more readily than the clinch knot when used with modern tippet materials.

Often a fine tippet will break at the first knot above the fly. Additional strength can be built into this knot by using a variation of the blood knot known as the Stu Apte improved blood knot, in which the smaller-diameter piece is doubled over before tying. Sometimes I regret becoming too lazy to use it consistently.

Anglers who fish this method are anything but casual practitioners of the sport. I would be surprised to find one who didn't possess an assortment of fly patterns that specifically imitate many of the common invertebrates that inhabit lakes. However, a good initial pattern is a small, weighted, light-toned nymph such as a size 14 or 16 Hare's-Ear Nymph, Otter Shrimp, or any olive mayfly nymph. These patterns could suggest scuds, water boatmen, caddis pupa, light-toned mayfly nymphs, or small dragonfly nymphs. A second selection might be something like a size 16 Sawyer's PT nymph or a Zug Bug to pass as a dark mayfly nymph, dark-cased caddis larva, or dark midge larva. Two specific patterns worth including due to their importance as trout food in many lakes are 1) midge pupa (i.e., size 16 to 20) and 2) damselfly nymphs (i.e., size 10 to 14).

11-1: *The slender silhouette of swimming mayfly nymphs suggests the use of Frank Sawyer's PT nymph. Compare the swept-back legs of this quiet-water insect with the sturdy legs of the crawling mayfly nymphs in figure 10-1.*

The color of the natural insect in lakes is often that of the background, whether it is aquatic vegetation or lake bottom. If a second trip is planned to the lake you are fishing, you may want to collect and photograph insects (before true color fades) in order to return with more realistic imitations of the trout's food.

When fishing deep your nymphs should be wrapped with anywhere from 6 to 10 turns of 1-amp lead wire. In fact, having some with six turns and others with 10 enables you to vary the depths you fish.

The Approach

This type of fishing can be done from a boat or float tube, while walking the banks, or while wading a shoreline. When wading, you should stalk the fish carefully, placing casts alongside shallow weedbeds and over the tops of those that lie deeper. Much of the previously covered material that dealt with approaching trout in lakes continues to hold true.

11-2: *When stalking fish among weedbeds, try to disturb the water as little as possible.*

In the absense of visible feeders, you often try to fish close to the bottom. The depth to fish can sometimes be estimated by studying the slope of the land above the waterline.

Casting Techniques

I use fewer casting variations with this method than with any other. It is probably because I need a well-executed overhead cast to obtain consistency in the turnover of unusually long leaders. In this turnover, I am not trying to straighten the tippet, because slack there contributes to a fast sink rate through the first half-dozen feet of water.

The casting adjustments I make are generally in response to windy conditions. The most common adjustments are those needed to cast into the wind—tilting the casting plane for lower forecasts and using additional rod butt in the casting stroke.

Line-Handling and Fishing Techniques

The best practitioners of this method are masters at retrieving the fly. Retrieves are sometimes based on careful study of the swimming movements of common lake insects (as observed in home aquariums), and developed by trial-and-error experimentation with various combinations of hand-twist or strip retrieves. Your movements of the artificial

11-3: *On a windy day, lake water moves and concentrates food along the leeward shore. Casting into the wind enables you to retrieve your fly with the current as if you are nymphing upstream.*

11-4: *Fishing a floating line with a rod tip held just above the surface simplifies line control.*

fly should be similar to those of the natural insect. The development of such retrieves may require the use of a swimming pool and a fishing buddy to cast and retrieve while you watch the fly's movements.

When nymphing in lakes, the retrieve possibilities with floating lines and long leaders are different than those with most sinking lines. Though you can sink the fly well below the surface with either type of line, the floating line enables you to retrieve with small up and down movements of the fly throughout the drift. This resembles the pre-emergence movement of mayfly nymphs and midge pupa. Most sinking lines, however, tend to drag the fly along behind in a relatively horizontal plane until late in the drift when the movement is upward toward the tip of the rod.

When the fly has reached a depth of 10 feet with a floating line, a distinct downward curve has formed throughout the leader. Where it disappears below the surface, the leader is relatively horizontal; where it attaches to the fly, its tippet is nearly vertical. This vertical drop of the tippet positions the fly in a vertical, head-up posture regardless of where the weight is placed on the shank of the hook.

So, when you strip in a few inches of line, the fly moves upward and slightly toward you. Between strips, the fly descends toward the bottom and again somewhat toward you. The deeper the fly, the more vertical this movement is.

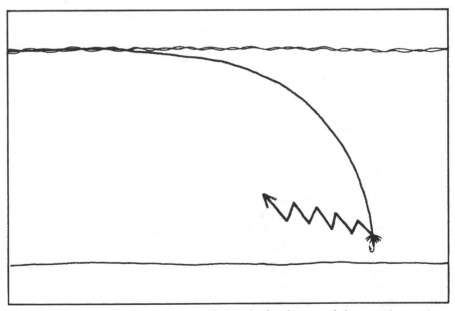

11-5: *A curve is formed in an unusually long leader that extends between floating line and weighted nymph. As you strip line, the fly moves upwards and toward you. Between strips, the fly drops but continues toward you.*

I mentioned that the depth you fish can be adjusted by varying the amount of weight on the nymph. It can be adjusted further by lengthening the tippet (for deeper drifts) or shortening it (for shallower drifts). Many anglers grease the leader butt instead of shortening the tippet, but Hal Janssen reports experiencing some spooking of fish by surface distortion created by the residue from the grease.

Hooking and Landing the Fish

In order to fish this method effectively, you must concentrate on the point at which your leader disappears into the water. If nothing happens, you begin to lose confidence and wonder if any fish are even in the area. For this reason, it is advisable to learn this method on a good, small lake, if one is available to you. At least then you know that trout are moving through the same piece of water you are casting into and fishing.

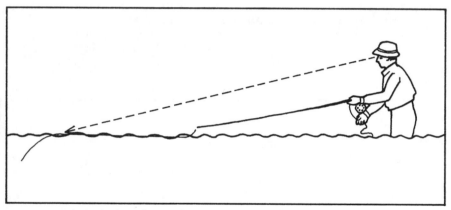

11-6: *Watch the leader where it disappears into the depths for the first indication of a trout's take.*

Quite often trout will take your fly while it is sinking, so any slowing or speeding in the sink rate of your leader is more likely to indicate a taking fish. At this time you should set the hook by raising the rod butt. A more vigorous technique could snap a tippet in this form of fishing. I have mentioned that a rod which is soft throughout its length seems to provide more cushioning against the shock of a strike (and your over-reaction) than does a relatively stiff-butted rod. The result is fewer breaks of 6X and 7X tippet material on the strike.

Trout in lakes sometimes grow to large sizes and can move with power and speed through still water. Such fish have potential to break the fine tippets by overrunning a low-quality reel. So for this method more than any other I have described, a relatively expensive, well-machined reel may become important.

Wading and Safety

When carefully stalking trout by wading soft-bottomed lakes, you sometimes stand in one spot for several minutes without being aware that you have sunk several inches into the silt. You soon learn to withdraw your foot carefully to avoid losing balance and falling.

Variations of this Method

Far more has been written about stream fly fishing than about lake fly fishing. It seems our knowledge of lakes has lagged behind, partly because of the difficulty of drawing generalizations from bodies of water that are so different from one another.

Solving the problem of attracting trout in lakes may include a consideration of the interplay of variables such as time of day, time of year, weather, equipment, casting adjustments, available trout food, retrieve variations, and characteristics of the lake itself. The possiblities seem endless, which of course, contribute to the challenge and fascination in this form of angling.

Selected References

Clarke, B. *The Pursuit of Stillwater Trout.* London: Adam and Charles Black, 1975.

Janssen, H. "Chironomidae: A Moveable Feast for Stillwater Trout," *Fly Fisherman*, 1981, Pre-Season.

Janssen, H. "Stillwater Secrets—Insects, Imitations and Fly Lines," in Scientific Anglers (Ed), *Fly Fishing Handbook.* Point Pleasant, N.J.: Aqua-Field, 1981.

Janssen, H. "The Basic Necessities," in J. Merwin (Ed.), *Stillwater Trout.* Garden City, New York, 1980.

Janssen, H. "The Nymph in Stillwater," in J. Merwin (Ed.). *Stillwater Trout.* Garden City, New York, 1980.

Raymond, S. "A Miscellaneous Bestiary," in J. Merwin (Ed.), *Stillwater Trout.* Garden City, New York, 1980.

12

BEYOND FLY FISHING METHODS

Adapting And Problem-Solving

Two years ago several friends joined me for an annual three-day fishing trip to the Sacramento and McCloud Rivers and Hat Creek. On that trip I didn't fish any differently than usual, but I did encounter more large fish that were willing to open their mouths at the wrong time. As a result I caught fish between 15 and 20 inches long on five of the methods described in this book. But I wasn't trying to catch fish on different methods. I was merely adapting my fishing to the variety of water I saw. And I think this *ability to adapt* is what differentiates the "hacker" from the expert and is what you should be working toward when you first practice fishing a method.

"Fishing a method" until you catch fish is an important process that enables you to gain confidence in a set of fly fishing techniques that is new to you. When you have confidence in your ability to use the techniques of that method, you are ready to incorporate it into your fishing repertoire and use it situationally in certain types of water. So when you practice fishing a given method, it's the method that determines the water you fish. But when you are adapting to the water being fished, it's the water that determines the method you select. It is subtleties of the water that call for adaptations which go beyond the method.

For example, let's imagine that you are about to fish a stream with pocket water. If you decide to fish a pocket-water method and you are in the early stages of learning it, you will repeat the same set of operations throughout the day, such as finding midstream rocks, positioning yourself, and casting into the slow water behind each one. You may even choose to pass up good water that doesn't suit a pocket-water method in order to concentrate on mastering one technique at a time and making it your own. However, as your basic pocket-water technique becomes more refined, you learn to vary the operations of fishing, such as the casting angles you select or the terminal rigging you use, in response to subtle differences among the pockets you fish. You have begun to consider the extent to which each pool is unique. So you even go so far as to develop distinctive fishing operations for each of your favorite pools and runs. By this time you have gone well beyond fishing a method.

Even the same piece of water must be fished differently at times. For instance, I remember well a day that my "program" didn't produce on one of my favorite runs at Hat Creek, where small dries or nymphs usually produce a fish or two for me. My good friend, Chet Murphy was across stream from me where he could see the two fish I was casting over. Occasionally he would inform me that the smaller fish had moved toward one of my size 16 nymphs or dry flies, but the larger fish continued to remain motionless two feet below the surface.

After half an hour, Chet suggested I try a large dry fly, because he had the impression that the small flies weren't drawing the trout's interest. Usually a large dry fly doesn't pay off during the midday hours at Hat Creek, but, because I was short on ideas, I tied on a size 10 Elk

Hair Caddis. The only large insects I had seen that morning were alder flies on some streamside foliage, so I blackened the caddis pattern with a felt pen. The larger fish, which hadn't moved a muscle for at least 30 minutes, rose quickly and surely to my first cast. Chet hung around long enough to make certain I returned his 15-inch "friend" to the stream.

Students often ask how I decide what methods or flies to use when first rigging-up for a day's fishing. If the stretch of water is known to me, I usually start at an "indicator pool" that I know holds trout. Assuming there is no appreciable surface feeding, I generally begin fishing there with a deep nymph. If a fish takes the fly decisively, my first indication is that the fish are active and thus vulnerable to whatever fly fishing method or technique seems best suited to the conditions. I may even be able to enjoy the scenery around me and catch fish without expending much energy (anglers are like trout). However, if I get only a faint "bump" or no strike at all, my first indication is that the fish are not active and that I should continue to fish my fly deep and cover the water thoroughly, using techniques and fly patterns described in Chapters 5 , 7 or 10. This fishing will require my complete concentration. Of course, each pool I fish either modifies or further confirms this first impression.

But what techniques or flies do I start with on water I haven't fished before? Though I may be influenced by rumors and information I have gathered about that water, I typically make my fishing decisions only after parting the last alder branches and viewing the water. If fish are neither rising nor visible, I do what most experienced fly fishers do— begin "searching" operations.

For me, searching consists of finding where the trout are, or ought to be, and surmising which flies they are most likely to take. I try to zero-in on the solution to these queries as quickly as possible, and use two types of techniques to do it—those that "double," in other words, cover two or more options, and those that permit quick rigging changes. Among the doubling techniques I have mentioned are selecting impressionistic flies that represent several types of insects and using two such flies at once to represent more insects and to sample two different depths simultaneously.

In some forms of doubling, the two (or more) options are covered on successive casts rather than on the same cast. Working up through a long run by alternating between short-line and long-line fishing is an example of this form of doubling. You may even select an initial stretch of stream that includes several types of water. This way you will sometimes find out quickly that trout are more active in certain types of water than in others. On lakes you may alternate between two different retrieves and use a "count" system to sample different depths.

I have also mentioned several techniques that permit you to change riggings quickly. I mentioned the loop system with interchangeable tippets to change weight, and extra reel spools or extra shooting tapers to change fly lines. The sooner you find where the fish are active and what they will take, the more time remains to fish effectively.

Sometimes that first glimpse of water reveals the presence of rising trout. While you no longer have to find active fish, you still must determine what fly they will take. This last part of the puzzle can be difficult to solve, particularly if the trout are taking only one stage (e.g., emerging nymphs) of one species of insect. What I do first in this situation is to watch the trout rise. If I see an insect, such as a floating mayfly, drifting downstream, I watch to see if it gets inhaled by a trout. If it does, I grab the next drifting mayfly, hold it on hand to examine the color of the underside of its body—the side the trout sees—and tie on a dry fly to match its size, shape, and color. This is the most direct form of "matching the hatch."

12-1: *Seeing trout take an insect off the surface creates excitement and solves problems.*

Even when you don't see an insect eaten, the way a trout rises can provide clues to its feeding. As Bob Dering puts it, you may then be able to "match flies to the rise." If a small bubble is visible after the rise or if you see the trout's mouth break through, it has taken something off the surface and can be caught on a dry fly. However, if you see only the back or tail of the rising fish, or the water merely swirls or "bulges," the chances are the trout is taking its food, such as emerging mayfly nymphs, just below the surface. When you see splashy, explosive rises, the trout is generally chasing fast-moving food, such as a minnow or an emerging caddis pupa. Quiet sipping by cruising fish, often in well-established patterns, suggests food that is small, abundant and vulnerable, such as tiny drifting mayfly "spinners" or midge pupa. A fish rising against a bank or under an overhanging tree or bush is often feeding on wind-blown land insects such as ants or grasshoppers.

12-2: *A trout changing position near the surface makes it tilt a little, which may appear as a sudden patch of light in dark water.*

It isn't always possible to tell from the "rise form" what a trout is eating, especially on broad stretches of water. So the next procedure I recommend is to wade downstream of the feeding trout without disturbing it and seine for drifting insects—"sift the drift." My seine is nothing more than a 12 by 18-inch piece of fine-mesh, fiberglass window screen with lengths of quarter-inch dowel rod taped to the shorter sides. This seine can be rolled up compactly until needed. I have found seining to be particularly enlightening when trout are taking food such a mayfly spinners and emerging pupae that are flush in the surface film and practically invisible to the naked eye.

Even your seine won't always solve the problem of what rising trout are eating. One day on the headwaters of the McCloud River, I was intrigued by a small trout that rose steadily in a quiet pool. I was still more intrigued after seining downstream of the fish without collecting so much as a single insect. I went back to fishing, without having solved the problem. Finally I caught that 9-inch trout—perhaps by irritating it. What I found was that it had been gorging on water boatmen, small water bugs that can rise vertically to get bubbles of air from the surface and swim back to their cover without being swept downcurrent to be inspected by cagey anglers.

A more typical stumbling-block to using a seine is the presence of deep, unwadable water downstream of the rising trout. Somehow it seems that every time deep water prevents me from using the seine, every visible insect is drifting well out of reach. With an esophagus pump, a suction device that samples the food a trout has just eaten, you may be able to "reveal the meal." These pumps can damage a trout fatally, though, unless used with very little suction. Of course, even a pump can't help is you haven't caught at least one of the rising fish.

So, observing rise forms, manipulating seine, using binoculars to watch drifting insects, and other "intelligence gathering" may leave you where you started—with no direct knowledge of what the trout are eating.

Resist for a little longer the urge to break the fly rod over your knee. The clues may have told you enough to select fly patterns logically—by the process of elimination. If you don't see upwing mayflies (duns) on the water, or if those you see are not being eaten, eliminate from consideration all your standard dry flies with upright wings. If some part of the fish is breaking the surface, eliminate weighted nymphs unless you are fishing them downstream and swinging them up to the surface. So your selection of flies has been limited to those designed to float down in the film—emerging nymphs and pupae and downwing dries such as adult caddis, mayfly spinners and adult stoneflies. The main thing I have found from checking the food eaten by evening-caught, meadow-stream trout is that these fish are selective, but not to the degree you might have expected. Their selectivity is frequently based on insect size and level of drift rather than particular species of insect. So the patterns I would start with in this situation are rather small (size 14 or 16) and fished in or just below the surface film. If this doesn't solve the problem, and you still aren't able to "deduce the abstruse," the time may have come to break that fly rod. Just don't break mine.

This subtle form of torture, matching the hatch, can become highly addictive. Many of the better players of this game are so addicted that they have uprooted themselves from city lives and found ways to reside close to noteworthy streams. Even if you are not driven to follow their example, you may want to get closer to the life of streams by taking up the study of aquatic entomology and relating that knowledge to fly tying. You can even bring the stream home with you by setting up an entomology aquarium to hatch out insect specimens for convenient observation. If the scientific side is not appealing, you can by-pass the study of insects and focus on specific fly hatches and use a limited number of well-established patterns. Many fly fishers use this approach at places like Henry's Fork in Idaho. They return each year at the same time when the patterns they successfully used in previous years should still be effective. If something has changed, they are quick to pounce on tackle shop owners and knowledgeable friends for the most current information and the "hot" patterns. They enjoy a sense of self-worth without having to spend much time delving into the intricacies of the sport.

Whether you have been matching the hatch for years or are looking forward to your first fly fishing trip, it's exciting to learn new things about fly fishing. Each stream or lake you visit, each day you string up a rod, and each trout that follows your fly has the potential to add something to your storehouse of knowledge and your pleasure. It is infinitely more exciting to me to catch a few fish by doing something new and different than to catch 50 or 100 trout doing something I already know.

I guess the most appealing thing to me about fly fishing is that there is so much to it. I have enjoyed learning to fly fish for 35 years and if fortunate enough to be fly fishing 35 years from now I will still be learning. Recently Scott Henderson jokingly asked me why I frequently put myself in the position of being outfished on "someone else's" stream. I answered that I like to learn new techniques and new waters, and don't mind even if my host takes the most productive spots. He knows the river and how to fish it most efficiently. Besides, the alternative is to bring him to my water, and use techniques I already know. I'd probably catch most of the fish that way, but I wouldn't learn much.

At this point, I'm looking forward to next season and that first day on the stream. I can't wait to find out what I don't know and what I'm going to learn next.